CARPOOLS TO CANDLELIGHT

EASY TO ELEGANT RECIPES

About the Artist

Grey Blackwell has been a newspaper artist/illustrator since 1992. He has also contributed artwork for such publications as Entertainment Weekly and MAD magazine. He trained at the School of Design at North Carolina State University and has been a member of the National Cartoonist Society since 1997. In 1998, he won the NCS Reuben Award for Newspaper Illustration. He is currently the graphics editor for the News and Observer in Raleigh, North Carolina.

For additional copies, contact:

Friends of St. Timothy's Hale School

3400 White Oak Road

Raleigh, North Carolina 27609

(919) 782-3331 ext. 503

ISBN: 0-9712774-0-0

November 2001   3,000 copies

Printed in the USA by

WIMMER

C O O K B O O K S

Memphis

1-800-548-2537

Carpools to Candlelight

You know the drill: drive here or there in your minivan, station wagon, SUV or sedan and wait in the carpool line. Out come the troops - your children, children of your friends, an assortment of young people - from band practice, soccer practice, basketball games, baseball games, volleyball, tennis - the list goes on and on. Into the car and off to the races!

It is the life story of each and every parent in every big city and small town. Whether you are heading home to a small apartment, a cozy brownstone, or a house in the suburbs, life with a family and children in middle and high school is like a crazy ride on a non-stop roller coaster. Keeping up with all the different schedules is a bit like being an air traffic controller - you have to make sure all the "flights" arrive and depart on time and that traffic keeps moving without collision or interruption.

And, if all of the homework and ball games and research papers and projects are not enough, there are still meals to prepare: snacks for starving teens; meals for hurried and harried families; luncheons for the volunteer group; parties for the office staff; special family events and holiday occasions; and even the occasional candlelight dinner!

We understand, which is why we put together a cookbook filled with both family food and fancy food. These are recipes carefully chosen from those our families and friends have enjoyed. You will find recipes for regular cooks, cooks in a hurry, gourmet cooks and gourmets at heart!

So, whether you are planning a tailgate party for football/hockey/soccer, a meal for family and friends, or a special dinner with the fancy china and the wedding crystal, we invite you and your busy family to enjoy the recipes that our busy families have put together and triple-tested for you.

We promise to have something for everyone -

from *Carpools to Candlelight!*

St. Timothy's ~ Hale School

St. Timothy's - Hale School is an independent Episcopal college preparatory school committed to high academic attainment in an atmosphere that emphasizes traditional Christian values, supportive environment, and small class sizes. Rigorous and demanding, the middle and upper school programs prepare its graduates for admission to an ever-growing number of colleges and universities. Outside of the classroom, students participate in extracurricular activities including athletics, drama, band, choir, clubs, student government, and honor council.

Located on 18 beautifully landscaped acres in suburban Raleigh, the School draws students from all parts of the Triangle, including Raleigh, Durham, Chapel Hill, Cary, Wake Forest, Garner, Knightdale, and other surrounding communities.

Friends of St. Timothy's ~ Hale School

Friends of St. Timothy's-Hale School is the parent support organization of St. Timothy's-Hale School in Raleigh, North Carolina. Since the founding of the school in 1972, the Friends organization has worked tirelessly to bring about parent participation and a closer relationship between the home and the school. "Friends" provides parent volunteers for many activities.

Previous fundraising efforts have provided improvements to the school library, faculty continuing education, technology equipment and software, science laboratories and equipment, furnishings for classrooms and administrative offices, athletic program enhancements, and programs and materials for the Fine Arts Department, as well as funding for special needs in all academic departments.

The proceeds from the sale of "Carpools to Candlelight" will help provide additional funds to continue our support of these and other enrichment programs.

Table of Contents

Denotes Quick and Easy Recipes

Denotes Elegant Recipes

When I was a child, my mother had the habit of fixing the same thing for dinner every night, for months and months at a time. I <u>promise</u> I'm not exaggerating.

During one phase, we had pecan waffles every night for <u>seven</u> months. We had the potato variety of "Hamburger Helper" every night for most of my sophomore year in high school!

I never realized this was odd until I was old enough to spend more than one night with a friend. Even then, I thought perhaps I was happening to visit during the two evenings when they were making the transition from one phase to the next.

I've never heard of another person who cooked this way!

Appetizers and Beverages

Accessible
to Brilliant

Appetizers

Beverages

Black Bean Dip

Preparation Time: 15 minutes ~ Cook Time: 10 minutes

1   14-ounce can black beans, mashed
1   10-ounce can sweet corn, drained
½   cup onions, chopped
1½ cups Cheddar cheese, shredded

½   cup salsa
Tortilla chips
Sour cream

- Fill bottom of a pie pan with mashed black beans. Top with corn, onion, then cheese.
- Bake at 375 degrees for 10 minutes. Let stand 5 minutes. Top with salsa and serve with chips and sour cream.

Serves: 6

Variations:

May substitute 3 ounces shredded Monterey Jack with jalapeños cheese and 3 ounces shredded sharp Cheddar cheese for the above cheese.

May add 4 ounces mild green chilies, chopped.

May add 4.25-ounce can sliced black olives.

Carolina Caviar

Preparation Time: 15 minutes, 2 hours refrigeration
Prepare ahead.

2   14-ounce cans black-eyed peas, drained
1   15-ounce can white hominy, drained
2   medium tomatoes, chopped
4   green onions, chopped
2   cloves garlic, minced
1   medium green pepper, chopped

1   jalapeño pepper, seeded, and chopped
½   cup onion, chopped
½   cup fresh parsley, chopped
1   8-ounce bottle Italian dressing
Tortilla chips

- Combine all ingredients except chips. Refrigerate 2 hours. Serve with tortilla chips.

Yield: about 5 cups

Creamy Cucumber Dip

Preparation Time: 15 minutes

---

16 ounces cream cheese, softened
2   tablespoons sour cream
1   clove garlic, crushed

1   large cucumber or 2 medium-size cucumbers
1   tablespoon fresh dill, chopped, optional

- Cream the softened creamed cheese and sour cream together with mixer until smooth. Stir in crushed garlic.

- Peel cucumber and grate into cream cheese mixture, adding dill if desired. Stir and chill. Serve with potato chips or vegetables.

Serves: 6 to 8

This also makes a good sandwich filling for tea sandwiches.

Guacamole

Preparation Time: 15 minutes
May prepare ahead.

---

5   avocados, peeled and mashed, reserving 1 pit
4   tablespoons onion, finely chopped
2   teaspoons salt
2   teaspoons Tabasco sauce

6   tablespoons mayonnaise
4   tablespoons lemon juice
1   tablespoon ketchup
½   teaspoon horseradish

- Combine all ingredients. Place pit in dip to prevent discoloring. Remove before serving.

- Serve with tortilla chips or as a side dish with Mexican entrée.

Yield: 1½ to 2 cups

Chesapeake Hot Crab Dip

Preparation Time: 15 minutes ~ Cook Time: 30 minutes
May prepare up to 8 hours ahead.

16 ounces cream cheese, softened	3 "shakes" of garlic salt
1 cup sour cream	2 green onions, finely chopped
4 heaping tablespoons mayonnaise (do not use Miracle Whip or low-fat mayonnaise)	1 pound fresh crabmeat
Juice of ½ lemon	½ cup sharp Cheddar cheese, finely grated and divided in half
3 teaspoons Worcestershire sauce	¼ cup plain, fine bread crumbs
1 teaspoon dry ground mustard	

- Combine first 8 ingredients. Mix until creamy. (Use the food processor to get the very best smooth texture.)

- Check through crabmeat for bits of shell. Then gently fold crabmeat and ¼ cup cheese into mixture. Spoon into 1½-quart casserole dish.

- Gently toss remaining ¼ cup cheese with bread crumbs and sprinkle lightly over casserole.

- Bake at 325 degrees for 30 minutes or until bubbly. Serve with crackers or toast points.

Serves: 15 to 20

To remove the odor of onions or garlic from your hands, rub them on anything made of stainless steel.

Real Texas Salsa

Preparation Time: 30 minutes
May prepare ahead.

---

2   14½-ounce cans stewed tomatoes
1   4-ounce can green chilies, chopped
1   medium onion, quartered
2-3 large garlic cloves, peeled
1-2 (depending on how hot you want it) fresh
      jalapeño, seeded

1-2 (depending on how hot you want it) red
      hot peppers, seeded
¼   cup fresh cilantro, chopped
¼   cup green onion, chopped
1   10-ounce can Rotel tomatoes
      Salt and pepper to taste

- Put all ingredients in food processor or blender. Blend until smooth. Refrigerate several hours before serving.
- Serve with tortilla chips or on assorted foods, such as baked potatoes, eggs, etc.

Yield: 3 pints

Water Chestnut Dip

Preparation Time: 15 to 20 minutes
May prepare ahead.

---

1   8-ounce can water chestnuts, chopped
      and drained
½   cup parsley, chopped
2   green onions, chopped
1   cup sour cream, may use "light"

1   cup mayonnaise, may use "light"
2   teaspoons Tabasco sauce
2   teaspoons soy sauce, may use "light"
      Raw vegetables, chips or crackers

- Combine first 7 ingredients and chill until firm. This may be done the day ahead of use.
- Serve with raw vegetables, chips or crackers.

Serves: 10

Roasted Red Pepper Hummus

Preparation Time: 10 minutes
Keeps in refrigerator for 2 weeks.

1	19-ounce can chickpeas, drained	3	cloves garlic, crushed, optional
2	tablespoons tahini	1	teaspoon cumin, optional
3	tablespoons lemon juice		Salt to taste
2	roasted red bell peppers		Wedges of pita bread
1	tablespoon olive oil		

- Mix first 7 ingredients in food processor. Season with salt. Chill.
- Serve with pita wedges.

Serves: 10 to 12

Variation: This can be made without the peppers. Add 2 more tablespoons tahini. Do not freeze.

Helpful Hint: 2 roasted red peppers are equivalent to a 7½-ounce jar of roasted red peppers.

Zesty Artichoke Dip

Preparation Time: 10 minutes ~ Cook Time: 15 to 20 minutes

1	14-ounce can artichoke hearts, drained and chopped	1	cup Parmesan cheese
1	4-ounce can chopped green chilies, not drained	1	cup mayonnaise

- Mix all of the ingredients. Spoon into lightly buttered baking dish (8 x 8-inch or 9 x 9-inch).
- Bake at 350 degrees for 15 to 20 minutes. Serve with tortilla chips.

Serves: 8

Almond Ham Rolls

Preparation Time: 30 minutes, freeze: 45 minutes

8	ounces cream cheese, softened	1	teaspoon Worcestershire sauce
¼	teaspoon dry mustard	2	teaspoons chives, chopped
¼	teaspoon paprika	2	tablespoons mayonnaise
3	dashes Tabasco sauce	1	tablespoon toasted almonds, chopped
	Dash salt and pepper	6	rectangular slices boiled ham
¼	teaspoon soy sauce		

- Mix cream cheese with all ingredients except ham, adding almonds last.

- Dry ham on paper towels. Spread 2 to 3 tablespoons cream cheese mixture on each slice of ham and roll lengthwise. Add a little mixture to the ends, if more filling is needed.

- Place in freezer for 45 minutes or until rolls are hard enough to slice. Cut into ½-inch rounds. Serve rounds with toothpicks or on crackers with a dash of mayonnaise, if desired.

Serves: 15 to 20

These may be wrapped and frozen for up to 4 weeks. Remove from freezer 1 hour before serving.

Bacon Crackers

Preparation Time: 15 minutes   ~   Cook Time: 40 minutes
May prepare ahead.

1	pound low-fat bacon	1	box captain's crackers

- Cut each slice of bacon into thirds. Wrap one piece around middle of each cracker. (Not too tightly.)

- Place on rack in pan (seam side down) in a 300-degree oven until brown, turn and cook until brown on both sides.

- Store in refrigerator or freezer. Serve at room temperature or slightly warm.

Serves: 10 to 12

These freeze beautifully and can be addictive!

East Indian Pâté

Preparation Time: 15 to 20 minutes
Prepare ahead: 4 hours

16 ounces cream cheese, softened	½ teaspoon salt
2 cups sharp Cheddar cheese, grated (room temperature)	1 8-ounce jar chutney (any flavor you like, mango chutney is good)
6 tablespoons sherry	½ cup peanuts or cashews, chopped
2 tablespoons Worcestershire sauce	½ cup green onion, chopped
1 teaspoon curry	½ cup coconut, grated

- Cream the cheeses with sherry, Worcestershire, curry, and salt. Line an 8-inch cake pan with plastic wrap, or lightly grease an 8-inch springform mold.

- Fill pan or mold with cheese mixture. Cover with plastic wrap and refrigerate for 4 hours.

- Unmold pâté on a large platter. Garnish in layers in this order: chutney, peanuts, onion, and coconut. Serve with crackers. Any crackers are good with this.

Serves: 24

May refrigerate up to 1 week.

Herb Garden Cheese Spread

Preparation Time: 15 minutes
Prepare ahead.

½ cup butter, softened	1 teaspoon each dried thyme, basil, marjoram, tarragon, and dill
1 teaspoon lemon juice	1 tablespoon parsley, chopped
8 ounces cream cheese, softened	1 tablespoon chives, chopped
1 clove garlic, minced	

- Whip butter and lemon juice together. Add cream cheese, herbs, and seasoning. Refrigerate until ready to serve.

- Serve at room temperature. Better made a day ahead. Serve with crackers or crostini.

Serves: 20

Four Cheese Pâté

Preparation Time: 45 minutes
Prepare ahead.

---

24 ounces cream cheese, softened, divided use
2 tablespoons milk
2 tablespoons sour cream
1 cup toasted pecans, chopped

1 4½-ounce package Camembert cheese, softened
1 4-ounce package crumbled blue cheese, softened
1 cup shredded Swiss cheese, softened

- Combine 8 ounces cream cheese, milk, and sour cream in a bowl. Beat with electric mixer on medium until smooth.

- Spread into a 9-inch pie plate lined with plastic wrap. Sprinkle with pecans.

- Combine remaining cream cheese with the Camembert, blue cheese, and Swiss cheese and beat until smooth with electric mixer. Spoon on top of pecans and spread to edge of pie plate.

- Cover with plastic wrap and chill. Will keep up to 1 week.

- To serve, invert onto serving plate and carefully peel away plastic wrap. Garnish with grape slices and parsley in a grape bunch design. Serve with assorted crackers.

Serves: 12 to 15

Mike Bailey's Cheese Ring

Preparation Time: 20 minutes
Prepare ahead.

---

2 cups extra sharp cheese, grated
¾-1 cup mayonnaise
1 cup nuts, chopped

1 cup onion, finely chopped
1 8 to 12-ounce jar raspberry preserves

- Combine cheese, mayonnaise, nuts, and onion. Mix well. Shape into ring. Hollow out center.

- Fill center with preserves. Chill to firm. Serve with crackers.

Serves: 8

Mushroom Pâté

Preparation Time: 20 minutes ~ Cook Time: 10 to 15 minutes
Best prepared a day ahead.

4   tablespoons butter at room temperature, divided use

8   ounces mushrooms, cleaned and finely chopped

1   teaspoon garlic, finely chopped

¼   cup scallions, white part only, finely chopped (about 1 bunch)

⅓   cup chicken broth

4   ounces cream cheese, at room temperature

Salt and pepper to taste

- Melt 2 tablespoons butter in medium-sized skillet over high heat. Add mushrooms and sauté 2 to 3 minutes. Add garlic and scallions and sauté 1 minute more. Add chicken broth and cook over high heat until all liquid has evaporated. Cool.

- Combine cream cheese and remaining 2 tablespoons butter. Add mushroom mixture, salt, and pepper. Mix well and refrigerate, ideally for 24 hours.

- Serve with crackers or baguette. Pretty with parsley and red peppers for garnish.

Yield: 1½ to 2 cups

Pistachio-Swiss Baguette

Preparation Time: 30 minutes
Prepare ahead.

1   cup Swiss cheese, grated

1   cup fresh Parmesan cheese, grated

½   cup (1 stick) unsalted butter, at room temperature

Heavy cream

½   cup blonde pistachios, coarsely chopped

1   loaf freshly made French baguette

- In a medium bowl or in a food processor (if available) blend the cheeses and butter well. Should be consistency of a thick paste. (Add heavy cream if too thick.) Stir in nuts.

- Slice the bread lengthwise into 2 to 3 sections. Remove soft bread inside. Stuff the cavities with the cheese nut mixture. Reform the loaf, wrapping snugly with plastic wrap. Chill.

- Serve by slicing into ½-inch slices. Delicious and different!

Serves: 6 to 12

Savory Cheesecake

Preparation Time: 30 minutes
Cook Time: 1 to 1¼ hours

1	refrigerator pie crust
2	cloves garlic
1	large onion, coarsely chopped
⅔	cup fresh parsley, chopped
3	ounces or ¾ cup Parmesan cheese, freshly grated
24	ounces cream cheese at room temperature
3	tablespoons all-purpose flour

4	large eggs
2	teaspoons salt
½	teaspoon Tabasco sauce
2	tablespoons fresh lemon juice
1	tablespoon fresh oregano, chopped
2	tablespoons fresh basil, chopped
½	tablespoon fresh rosemary, chopped
½	cup pepperoni, chopped

- Evenly press pie crust on the bottom and sides of an 8-inch springform pan.

- Chop garlic in food processor; add onion, then parsley and Parmesan cheese. Add cream cheese, 8 ounces at a time and process. Add flour and 1 egg and continue processing until smooth.

- Add remaining 3 eggs, one at a time, blending well after each addition. Add salt, Tabasco, lemon juice, and herbs, processing just until blended. Stir in pepperoni and pour into dough-lined pan.

- Bake at 400 degrees for 10 minutes, then reduce heat to 325 degrees and bake 50 minutes longer or until the cake is set. Let cool and remove from springform pan.

- Refrigerate until ready to use. Serve cheese spread on crackers, using the pie crust as your serving dish!

Serves: 12 to 15

Tuna Pâté Italiano

Preparation Time: 10 minutes
Prepare at least 2 hours ahead.   ~   Freezes well.

1	16-ounce can tuna, drained
8	ounces cream cheese
2	anchovy filets

1	teaspoon capers with juice
1	teaspoon lemon juice

- Puree all ingredients in food processor. Refrigerate for 2 to 24 hours.
- Remove from refrigerator 2 hours before serving. Serve with crackers.

Yield: 1½ cups

Smoked Salmon Pâté

Preparation Time: 10 minutes   ~   Prepare several hours ahead.

8	ounces cream cheese
¼	pound smoked salmon
1	tablespoon lemon juice

¾	tablespoon onion, minced
½	tablespoon parsley, chopped fine
¼	teaspoon garlic powder

- Mix all ingredients in food processor. Serve with crackers.

Yield: 1½ cups

Stuffed Spinach Mushrooms

Preparation Time: 20 minutes ~ Cook Time: 15 to 18 minutes

24	large mushroom caps	2	teaspoons lemon juice
2	tablespoons butter, melted	1	teaspoon instant minced onion
1	package frozen spinach soufflé (thawed)	½	teaspoon salt
1	cup bread crumbs, not toasted		Parmesan cheese, grated

- Place mushroom caps on well-greased baking sheet and brush with melted butter.

- Mix spinach, bread crumbs, lemon juice, onions, and salt. Divide evenly and stuff each mushroom cap.

- Sprinkle with Parmesan cheese. Bake at 350 degrees for 15 to 18 minutes.

Yield: 6 to 8 servings

Parmesan Stuffed Mushrooms

Preparation Time: 15 minutes ~ Cook Time: 15 minutes

¼	cup grated Parmesan cheese, grated	2	tablespoons olive oil
½	cup flavored bread crumbs	24	large mushroom caps
			Butter

- Mix cheese, bread crumbs, and oil. Arrange mushrooms in shallow well-greased pan.

- Fill mushroom caps with mixture and place a sliver of butter on top of each.

- Bake at 350 degrees for 15 minutes or until lightly browned.

Yield: 6 to 8 servings

Asparagus Pinwheels

Preparation Time: 1 hour ~ Cook Time: 15 minutes
May prepare ahead.

---

20 slices thin soft white bread
3 ounces blue cheese
8 ounces cream cheese, softened
1 egg

20 fresh asparagus spears, pencil-thin, blanched
¼ pound butter, melted

- Trim bread and flatten slightly. Blend blue cheese, cream cheese, and egg. Spread on slices of bread.

- Roll one asparagus spear in each slice, dip in butter. Place on cookie sheet and then in freezer. Continue process until all rolls are frozen. Do NOT leave in freezer.

- Slice each roll into 3 pieces. Bake at 400 degrees for 15 minutes or until lightly browned.

Yield: 60 pieces

Blanched asparagus-Place asparagus in boiling water for 5 to 7 minutes until color brightens. Plunge asparagus immediately into ice water bath. Continue with remainder of recipe. This is a good way to prepare vegetables for pasta salads and other recipes that call for fresh, crisp-cooked vegetables.

Confetti Shrimp

Preparation Time: 45 minutes
Prepare ahead.

---

2 pounds medium shrimp, cooked, peeled, and deveined
1 Vidalia onion, quartered and thinly sliced
¼ cup rice wine vinegar
⅓ cup light olive oil
¼ cup fresh lemon juice
1 red bell pepper, finely diced
1 yellow pepper, finely diced

1 clove garlic, minced
1 tablespoon fresh parsley, chopped
1 tablespoon fresh basil, chopped
1 tablespoon fresh chives, chopped
1 teaspoon fresh thyme
1 teaspoon sugar
1 teaspoon salt
1 teaspoon ground black pepper

- Combine shrimp and onions in a bowl. Combine remaining ingredients and toss with shrimp and onions.

- Cover and chill at least 1 hour, longer is better.

Serves: 10

Hot Crab Toasts

Preparation Time: 20 minutes ~ Cook Time: 10 minutes
May be prepared ahead.

---

1 5-ounce jar of Old English cheese spread
½ cup butter, softened
1 7½-ounce can crabmeat, rinsed in cold water and drained

1 tablespoon Worcestershire sauce
¼ teaspoon garlic salt
6 English muffins, halved

- Blend butter and cheese, then add crabmeat, Worcestershire sauce, and garlic salt. Divide mixture among the 12 muffin halves, spreading onto each. Cut each half into eighths.

- Freeze in 1 layer on a cookie sheet. Transfer to a large plastic freezer bag and store in the freezer. Remove from freezer and bake at 450 degrees for 10 minutes, as needed.

Yield: 96 bites

Grilled Bacon-Wrapped Shrimp

Preparation Time: 20 minutes, marinate 1 to 2 hours
Cook Time: 6 to 10 minutes

Hickory, apple or cherry wood chips
½ cup soy sauce
1 tablespoon brown sugar
1 tablespoon dry sherry
1 large clove garlic, crushed
Dash Worcestershire sauce

Dash cayenne pepper
Small piece fresh ginger root peeled and crushed
1 pound large shrimp, shelled, deveined, leaving tail intact
8 slices lean bacon

- Cover wood chips with water and soak for 30 minutes.

- Combine all ingredients except shrimp and bacon. Cook over moderate heat to blend flavors and set aside for 1 hour.

- Cut bacon slices into one-thirds. Wrap a piece of bacon around each shrimp and skewer to secure. Pour marinade over shrimp and chill for 1 to 2 hours.

- Remove from marinade and grill over hot coals and wood chips for 6 to 10 minutes, turning once. Do not overcook.

Serves: 8

Marinated Shrimp in Fresh Dill

Preparation Time: 20 minutes ~ Cook Time: about 5 minutes to cook shrimp
Prepare ahead.

2½ pounds boiled shrimp, peeled
½ cup olive oil
½ cup dry white wine
4 teaspoons fresh dill, chopped
1 teaspoon fresh pepper

Dash garlic powder
2 drops hot sauce
½ cup lemon juice
Salt to taste
2 tablespoons fresh chives, chopped

- Place shrimp in a glass bowl. Combine the remaining ingredients and pour over shrimp. Marinate overnight in refrigerator.

Serves: 8 to 10

Party Meatballs

Preparation Time: 30 minutes ~ Cook Time: 60 minutes
May prepare ahead.

1½ pounds ground beef	1½ teaspoons salt
½ cup dry bread crumbs	¼ teaspoon pepper
½ cup milk	¼ teaspoon garlic salt
1 egg, beaten	1 cup chili sauce
¼ cup onion, minced	1 cup whole cranberry sauce

- Combine all ingredients except chili and cranberry sauces, and shape into meatballs. Place in shallow baking pan and brown in 350 degree oven for 30 minutes. Drain off fat.

- Pour chili and cranberry sauces over meatballs and bake 30 minutes. Serve on party tray with toothpicks.

Serves: 12 to 15

To prepare ahead and freeze: Bake meatballs. Freeze in freezer bags. When ready to use, thaw. Place in baking pan, cover with chili and cranberry sauces and bake at 350 degrees for 30 to 40 minutes.

Olive Bites

Preparation Time: 20 minutes ~ Cook Time: 8 to 10 minutes

1 small loaf French bread, cut into ¼-inch slices	1 bunch green onions, finely chopped
1 4.25-ounce can chopped black olives	½ cup grated Parmesan cheese
	¾ cup mayonnaise

- Lightly toast French bread slices on one side.

- Mix remaining ingredients together. Spread on untoasted side of bread and cook under broiler until browned and bubbly. Serve immediately.

Serves: 8 to 10

Spinach Balls

Preparation Time: 20 minutes, additional time for chilling
Cook Time: 30 minutes

2	10-ounce packages frozen chopped spinach, thawed and drained well	4	eggs
2	cups seasoned dressing mix	1	small onion, grated
¾	cup butter, melted	½	teaspoon thyme
½-¾	cup Parmesan cheese, grated	½	teaspoon salt
		½	teaspoon garlic salt

- Mix all ingredients together and chill for several hours.
- Roll into balls about the size of a walnut. Place in a 9 x 13-inch baking dish coated with cooking spray.
- Bake at 350 degrees for 30 minutes. Serve immediately.

Serves: 12

Southern Baked Brie

Preparation Time: 20 minutes ~ Cook Time: 30 minutes

1	8-inch round Brie cheese	½	pound bacon, cooked, and crumbled
½	cup brown sugar	½	cup green onions, tops included, chopped
⅓	cup pecan pieces		

- Place Brie in an ovenproof dish. Crumble brown sugar and pecans on top, to within 1 inch of the edge of the Brie.
- Bake at 350 degrees for 30 minutes. Remove from oven and top with green onions and bacon. Serve hot with crackers of choice.

Serves: 16 to 20

Variations: Use 1 cup chutney or 1 10-ounce jar red raspberry jelly instead of brown sugar and pecan mixture.

Rosemary Nuts

Preparation Time: 20 minutes ~ Cook Time: 10 minutes
May prepare ahead.

1   pound unsalted whole cashews
2   tablespoons fresh rosemary, chopped
½   teaspoon cayenne pepper

2   teaspoons dark brown sugar
2   teaspoons kosher salt
1   tablespoon butter, melted

- Spread nuts evenly on baking sheet and toast for 10 minutes in oven at 350 degrees.

- In large bowl mix rest of ingredients while nuts are in oven. Toss nuts in mixture while hot. Cool before serving.

Serves: 8

Very Tasty Roses

Preparation Time: 60 minutes ~ Cook Time: 10 minutes

1   package fresh or frozen won ton wrappers or egg roll wrappers, cut in fourths
2   tablespoons olive oil
2   cups (1 pound) sausage, cooked and crumbled
½   cup green onions, chopped
1½ cups red, yellow, and green peppers, chopped

½   cup tomatoes, chopped
1   4.25-ounce can sliced black olives
½   cup mozzarella cheese, grated
½   cup feta cheese, grated
1   tablespoon fresh basil, chopped
    Salt and pepper to taste

- Lightly grease a mini or regular muffin tin. Press 1 wrapper into each cup. Brush with olive oil. Bake for 5 minutes at 350 degrees until golden. Remove from tin and place on cookie sheet.

- For filling, heat oil and sauté the sausage, onions, and peppers for 3 to 4 minutes. Remove from heat and add tomatoes, olives, mozzarella, feta, basil, and season to taste with salt and pepper. Mix well.

- Fill wrappers with sausage mixture and bake 5 minutes at 350 degrees until bubbly. Serve immediately.

Yield: 4 to 5 dozen mini muffins or 2 dozen in regular size muffins

Sweet Peppers and Cheese Puffs

Preparation Time: 15 minutes ~ Cook Time: 20 minutes
May prepare ahead.

1   17.3-ounce package frozen puff pastry sheets, 2 pastry sheets per package
    2 red peppers, chopped

2   yellow peppers, chopped (use green peppers at Christmas)

1   8-ounce block of Cheddar cheese

- Spread out 1 pastry sheet in bottom of a 9 x 13-inch baking pan. Place peppers evenly over pastry.

- Put thick slices of Cheddar cheese in strips on top of peppers. Put second pastry sheet on top of cheese to cover.

- Bake 20 minutes at 400 degrees. Allow to cool, and cut into diagonal pieces.

Serves: 8 to 10

Southern Mint Tea

1   quart boiling water

6   individual or regular-size tea bags

1   cup sugar (also good with sugar substitute)

    Juice of 2 lemons

1   cup mint leaves

1   quart cold water

- In boiling water steep tea bags, sugar, lemon juice, and mint for 10 minutes or until desired strength.

- Add cold water. Remove tea bags and mint. Serve over ice.

Yield: 2 quarts

Hot Cinnamon Cranberry Punch

Freezes well.

2½ quarts water, divided use
2½ cups sugar
1 cup red-hot cinnamon candies

12 whole cloves
2 quarts cranberry juice
2 6-ounce cans frozen orange juice, thawed

- Boil 1 quart water with the sugar, red-hots, and cloves. Remove cloves and add juices.
- Stir in remaining 1½ quarts water. Serve hot.

Serves: 20

Summertime Punch

---

3 cups sugar (add additional sugar if needed for taste, later)
10 cups water
1 large can unsweetened pineapple juice

1 43-ounce container fresh orange juice, not canned
12 ounces bottled lemon juice (1½ cups)
3 2-liter bottles ginger ale

- Dissolve sugar in water. Add juices. This can be frozen in containers or ziplock bags.
- Mix with the ginger ale when ready to serve.

Serves: 50

After Dinner Iced Coffee

½ ounce Kahlúa
½ ounce Irish Mist
½ ounce Bailey's Irish Cream

2 ounces espresso coffee
Crushed ice

- Mix all ingredients in the order given. Stir well. Pour into an old-fashioned glass and serve.

Serves: 1

"Who Made the Punch?" Punch

3 6-ounce cans frozen lemonade concentrate, undiluted	1 46-ounce can orange juice
2 46-ounce cans pineapple juice	2 tablespoons almond extract
8 6-ounce cans water	2 tablespoons vanilla extract
	2 liters ginger ale, chilled

- Combine all ingredients, except the ginger ale, in a large bowl or pot and chill.
- Transfer to a punch bowl just before serving and add the ginger ale.

Yield: 4 quarts

Variation: This also makes a delicious cocktail. Simply add 1 cup of Amaretto liqueur and freeze to a slushy consistency. Great to serve at parties!

Reception Punch

1 quart cranberry juice cocktail	½ cup sugar
1 pint pineapple juice	1½-2 liters ginger ale

- Mix cranberry juice, pineapple juice, and sugar. Freeze in a ziplock bag until slushy. Add ginger ale to taste.
- May be frozen ahead and thawed to slush before adding ginger ale.

Serves: 20

This punch is a very festive red color.

Frozen Whiskey Sours

1   6-ounce can frozen lemonade concentrate   **Bourbon, to fill can**
    Water, to fill can   **Lemon slices or cherries**

- Combine lemon concentrate with water and bourbon. Mix and freeze to a slushy consistency. Use a covered container, allowing for expansion.
- Stir every 2 to 3 hours. Serve in cocktail glasses with a cherry and/or a lemon slice.

Serves: 4 to 6

Variation: For lime daiquiris, substitute limeade for lemonade and rum for bourbon.

Coffee Punch

½   **gallon strong coffee**   ½   **gallon vanilla ice cream, softened**
1   **cup sugar**

- Make coffee according to directions for your coffeepot. (If using Mr. Coffee, 12 cups equal ½ gallon.)
- Transfer hot coffee to a container and add sugar. Stir until sugar dissolves and put sweetened coffee into refrigerator until well chilled (can be made a day or two ahead.)
- Put softened ice cream into punch bowl and cut into chunks. Pour coffee over ice cream and serve.

Serves: 16

Wassail

1	cup sugar	½	cup lemon juice
4	cinnamon sticks	2	cups pineapple juice
½	cup water	1½	cups white wine
2	cups orange juice		Lemon slices
6¼	cups good jug Burgundy wine		

- Make syrup by boiling sugar and cinnamon sticks in water for 5 minutes and strain. Set aside.

- Heat, but do no boil, the remaining ingredients. Combine with syrup, garnish with lemon slices and serve simmering.

Serves: 12

Champagne Reception Punch

5	bottles Champagne	1	cup sugar
2	bottles cognac	1	block ice
3	packages frozen pineapple, defrosted	3	quarts sparkling water

- Chill all liquors and at serving time dissolve sugar in defrosted pineapple in bottom of punch bowl. Add the block of ice, the liquors, and the sparkling water. Stir.

Serves: 20

Raspberry Champagne Punch

2　10-ounce packages frozen red raspberries in syrup, slightly thawed
⅓　cup lemon juice from concentrate
½　cup sugar

1　750 ml bottle red rosé wine, chilled
1　quart raspberry sorbet or sherbet
1　750 ml bottle Aste Spumanti or champagne, chilled

- Puree raspberries in a blender.

- Combine pureed raspberries, lemon juice, sugar, and wine in a large punch bowl. Stir just until sugar dissolves.

- Just before serving, scoop sherbet into punch bowl and add champagne. Stir gently.

Serves: 12

Mint Juleps

1　cup sugar
⅔　cup water
¼　teaspoon cream of tartar
　　Fresh mint (enough for a sprig for each glass plus 3 bruised sprigs)

Crushed ice
Bourbon, 1½ to 2 jiggers per drink (1 jigger equals 1½ ounces)

- Combine sugar, water, and cream of tartar in a saucepan. Cook over low heat, stirring with a wooden spoon until hot and most of the sugar is dissolved.

- Bring to a simmer, cover, and continue to simmer for 2 minutes. Remove from heat.

- Bruise 3 sprigs of mint and drop into sugar syrup. Let cool.

- Fill a silver cup with crushed ice. Add 1 to 2 tablespoons of sugar syrup. Add 1½ to 2 jiggers of good bourbon and 1 sprig of mint.

Serves: 6

Rosé Sparkle Punch

Preparation Time: 1 hour and 15 minutes

4 **10-ounce packages frozen strawberries, thawed**
1 **cup sugar**
4 **bottles rosé wine, divided use**

4 **6-ounce cans frozen lemonade concentrate, thawed**
2 **750 ml bottles sparkling water**
Block ice

- In a bowl, combine strawberries, sugar, and 1 bottle of wine. Cover and let stand at room temperature 1 hour.

- Strain mixture into a punch bowl. Add frozen lemonade; stir. Add remaining 3 bottles of wine, and stir in sparkling water.

- Add block of ice at serving time.

Serves: 20 to 24

For a festive touch, float gardenia blooms in the punch bowl.

Irish Cream

1¾ **cups bourbon or brandy**
1 **14-ounce can sweetened condensed milk**
1 **cup whipping cream or light cream**
4 **eggs**

2 **tablespoons chocolate syrup**
2 **teaspoons instant coffee**
1 **teaspoon vanilla**
½-1 **teaspoon almond extract**

- Combine all ingredients in blender. Blend until smooth. Keeps in refrigerator for 1 month.

Serves: 6

Hummingbird Nectar

3	cups water	1	cup sugar

- Boil sugar and water for 4 minutes. Cool and fill feeder.
- Refrigerate the rest for future use.

Yield: 3 cups

Magnolia Blossoms

1 6-ounce can frozen orange juice, thawed	Sugar to taste
3 cups Chablis wine	Crushed ice
1½ cups water	Orange slices for garnish
½ cup triple sec	

- Mix first 5 ingredients together and chill. Serve over ice in wine glasses and garnish with orange slices.

Serves: 8

Salads

Simple to
Sensational

Salads

Marinated Artichoke Salad

Preparation Time: 30 minutes

1   package chicken Rice-a-Roni, prepared as directed
6   green onions, chopped
½   cup red bell pepper, chopped
⅓   cup mayonnaise

10 green olives with pimentos, sliced
¼   teaspoon curry powder
2   10-ounce jars marinated artichoke hearts, chopped (reserve marinade)

- Mix all ingredients including the marinade.

- Chill. Best if prepared one or more days ahead.

Serves: 6

Variation: 2 cups of cooked chopped chicken breasts may be added to become an entrée salad.

Mediterranean Artichoke Salad

Preparation Time: 15 to 20 minutes

1   14-ounce can artichoke hearts, quartered and drained
1   14.4-ounce can hearts of palm, cut into ½-inch slices and drained
1   3.8-ounce can sliced black olives, drained

1   2-ounce jar chopped pimento, drained
1   3.5-ounce container feta cheese
1   medium onion, chopped
1   8-ounce bottle Newman's Italian Dressing

- Combine first 4 ingredients. Crumble feta cheese over vegetables.

- Add onion to vegetables. Sprinkle Newman's Italian Dressing over mixture and toss.

Serves: 8

Asparagus and Goat Cheese Salad

Preparation Time: 15 minutes

1 pound pencil thin asparagus, trimmed and cut into 1½-inch length

2 tablespoons cider vinegar

½ teaspoon salt

½ teaspoon freshly ground pepper

¼ cup plus 2 tablespoons safflower or canola oil

1 large head of Boston lettuce

2 ounces dry goat cheese, chilled

- In a medium skillet, bring 1 inch of lightly salted water to a boil over high heat. Add asparagus and cook briefly (30 seconds to 1 minute). Drain and let cool.

- In a medium bowl, whisk the vinegar with the salt and pepper. Pour in the oil in a thin stream, whisking until mixed. Add asparagus and toss to coat.

- Mound lettuce on 6 salad plates. Spoon the asparagus and dressing over the lettuce and crumble the goat cheese on top.

Serves: 6

If prepared a day early, add a dash of lemon juice to asparagus to keep color. Don't put on lettuce until serving.

Hawaiian Broccoli and Cauliflower Salad

Preparation Time: 30 minutes

5 cups cauliflower, broccoli or combination of both

¼ cup onion, chopped

½ cup raisins

½ cup vinegar

8 strips bacon, crumbled

3 tablespoons prepared mustard

1 14-ounce can (or less) Eagle Brand milk

½ teaspoon salt

½ teaspoon pepper

- Combine all ingredients. Toss and serve chilled.

Serves: 6 to 8

Asian Nutty Salad

Preparation Time: 30 minutes

Salad

½	cup butter or margarine	1	head Napa cabbage
½	cup sunflower seed centers	1	head romaine lettuce
½	cup slivered almonds	4	scallions, chopped
2	packages Ramen noodles (no spice packet)	1	11-ounce can Mandarin oranges

Dressing

½	cup safflower oil	¼	cup white or cider vinegar
⅓	cup sugar		Pinch salt
1	tablespoon soy sauce		

- Sauté seeds, nuts, and noodles in butter until brown, about 20 minutes. Add to salad mixture of cabbage, lettuce, scallions, and oranges.

- Combine dressing ingredients and toss with salad.

Serves: 8

Delicious with Chinese Pork Tenderloin or Flank Steak Teriyaki!

Crispy Hot Chicken Salad

Preparation Time: 30 minutes

2 cups chicken breasts, diced and cooked	2 teaspoons onion, grated
2 cups celery, very thinly sliced	2 teaspoons lemon juice
½-¾ cup Cheddar cheese, grated	¾-1 cup mayonnaise
½ cup almonds, sliced and toasted	(not reduced-fat mayonnaise)
½ teaspoon salt	1 cup potato chips, crushed

- Mix all ingredients with the exception of the chips.

- Divide into sixths and form into balls. Roll balls in chips. Place on a greased baking sheet and bake at 375 degrees for 15 to 20 minutes.

Serves: 6

Broccoli Salad

Preparation Time: 15 to 20 minutes

Salad

2 bunches broccoli, cut to florets	1 pound bacon, cooked crisp and crumbled
1½ cups raisins	⅓ cup red onion, optional
⅓ cup pecans or sunflower seeds	

Dressing

1½ cups mayonnaise	3 tablespoons white vinegar
3 tablespoons sugar	

- Toss broccoli, raisins, nuts or seeds, and bacon in a large bowl, adding onion if desired.

- For dressing, combine mayonnaise, sugar, and white vinegar. Toss gently with broccoli mixture. Chill and serve.

Serves: 8

For dressing, may use ¼ cup clear corn syrup instead of sugar and ½ cup less mayonnaise.

Copper Pennies Carrot Salad

Preparation Time: 15 to 20 minutes
Cook Time: 10 to 15 minutes

2 pounds carrots, peeled and cut into disk shapes	1 teaspoon Worcestershire sauce
1 can tomato soup	½ teaspoon salt
½ cup vegetable oil	¼ teaspoon pepper
⅔ cup sugar	1 medium onion, chopped or sliced, optional
¾ cup vinegar	1 medium green pepper, chopped or sliced, optional
1 teaspoon dry mustard	

- Boil carrots until tender, 10 to 15 minutes.

- In a separate pan, cook remaining ingredients and bring to a boil. Simmer 10 minutes, cool.

- Pour over carrots. Refrigerate and keep up to 2 months.

Serves: 6 to 8

Crab Salad

Preparation Time: 30 minutes

2 cups cooked pasta (you can use shells, elbows)	1 cup celery, chopped
1 can crabmeat, rinsed thoroughly in cold water and drained	1 medium onion, chopped
	½ cup mayonnaise

- Mix together ingredients and refrigerate for 1 hour (or more).

Serves: 4

Any other vegetables can be used for color (peppers, radishes, etc.)

Chinese Chopped Chicken Salad

Preparation Time: 20 minutes

1   head lettuce, chopped
3   green onions, chopped
1   sweet red pepper, chopped
6   ounces fresh or frozen (thawed) snow peas
2   cups chopped chicken
1   3-ounce package spicy flavored instant ramen soup mix

¼   cup rice vinegar
1   tablespoon soy sauce
1   tablespoon sesame oil
6   tablespoons peanut oil
    Salt and pepper to taste
2   tablespoons sesame seeds, toasted

- Combine lettuce, onions, red pepper, pea pods, and meat. Crumble dry noodles from soup over vegetables.

- Combine seasoning package from the soup with vinegar and soy sauce in a small bowl. Whisk in oils, salt, and pepper.

- Pour dressing over vegetable mix. Add sesame seeds and toss.

Serves: 6 to 8

Variations: May use turkey, pork, or shrimp instead of the chicken. Also may substitute olive oil for sesame oil.

Chicken is more easily skinned and boned if slightly frozen.

Cold Chicken and Pasta Salad

Preparation Time: 45 minutes plus 1 hour refrigeration time

3	cups chicken broth	½	teaspoon Dijon mustard
3	chicken breast halves, skinned and boned	2	celery ribs, stringed, cut crosswise into approximately ⅛-inch slices
5	ounces shell-shaped pasta		
1	cup nonfat mayonnaise	1	cup baby spring peas, cooked briefly
½	teaspoon celery salt	1	cup seedless red grapes, washed, dried, and halved
½	teaspoon fresh ground black pepper		

- Bring chicken broth to a boil over medium-high heat in a medium-sized saucepan. Add chicken breasts, turn heat to low and simmer gently for 20 minutes. Cool. Remove chicken and chill.

- Save defatted broth to cook pasta in. Add enough water to broth to bring volume to 1 quart. Cook shells according to package. Drain, rinse under cold water. Set aside.

- Whisk together mayonnaise, celery salt, pepper, and mustard in medium mixing bowl. Cut chicken breasts into bite-sized pieces. Add to pasta, celery, peas, and grapes.

- Stir and toss to combine. Cover and refrigerate for 1 hour.

Serves: 6

Greek Chicken Salad

Preparation Time: 1 hour

3	cups chicken breast, cooked and cubed	1½	cups ruffled pasta, uncooked
2	medium cucumbers, peeled, seeded and chopped (dry with a paper towel)	3	garlic cloves, minced or pressed
		½	cup plain yogurt
¾-1¼	cups crumbled feta cheese	½	cup mayonnaise
⅔	cups sliced pitted black olives	1	tablespoon dried leaf oregano
¼	cup fresh parsley, chopped		

- Combine chicken, cucumbers, feta cheese, olives, and parsley in a bowl. Cook and drain pasta according to package directions.

- For the dressing, combine the garlic, yogurt, and mayonnaise and mix well. Add garlic dressing and pasta to the other mixture. Add oregano last and toss.

Serves: 8

Flavors blend when made a day or a few hours ahead.

Cranberry-Orange Relish

Preparation Time: 20 minutes

---

1   quart or 1 pound fresh cranberries,
        washed and sorted

2   oranges, quartered and seeded
2   cups sugar

- Put all ingredients in a food processor and add sugar.
- Keeps in refrigerator for several weeks. Can be frozen for later use.

Yield: about 1 quart

Great as a condiment with poultry!

Wild Rice and Chicken Salad

Preparation Time: 30 to 45 minutes plus 2 to 3 hours refrigeration time
Prepare ahead.

---

1   6-ounce box long grain and wild rice
4   chicken breasts, stewed, skin and bone
        removed
1   cup red seedless grapes, cut in half
1   cup celery, chopped
1   cup cashews, coarsely chopped

2   tablespoons onion, finely chopped
½   teaspoon salt
1   cup mayonnaise (lite or regular)
1   tablespoon milk
3   tablespoons lemon juice

- Prepare rice according to package directions and refrigerate until chilled.
- Cut cooked chicken into cubes and combine with grapes, celery, cashews, onion, and chilled rice.
- In small bowl combine salt, mayonnaise, milk, and lemon juice. Pour mayonnaise mixture over chicken mixture and mix to combine.
- Refrigerate 2 to 3 hours or overnight before serving.

Serves: 8 to 10

Corn and Black Bean Salad

Preparation Time: 20 minutes

Salad

1	16-ounce can black beans, rinsed and drained	½	cup red pepper strips
2	cups frozen corn, thawed	½	cup scallions, chopped
1	cup celery, chopped	3	tablespoons cilantro (or more, to taste), chopped

Dressing

3	tablespoons balsamic vinegar	½	teaspoon salt
2	teaspoons honey	¼	cup olive oil
1½	teaspoons Dijon mustard	3	tablespoons vegetable oil
1	clove garlic, pressed or minced	⅛	teaspoon pepper

- Combine beans, corn, celery, pepper strips, and scallions.
- For dressing, blend ingredients.
- Combine salad mixture with dressing, and add cilantro when ready to serve.

Serves: 8 to 10

 # Tomato-Basil Bow Tie Salad

Preparation Time: 20 minutes

1	pound plum tomatoes, chopped (2 cups)	2-3	cloves garlic, minced
⅓	cup fresh basil, cut in thin slices	1	teaspoon salt
1	tablespoon olive oil	6	ounces bow tie pasta, cooked and drained
1	tablespoon red wine vinegar		Dash ground pepper

- In a large bowl combine first 6 ingredients. Add cooked bow ties and toss to combine.
- Sprinkle with pepper. Serve warm or at room temperature.

Serves: 6

Greek Rice Salad

Preparation Time: 40 minutes ~ Cook Time: 20 minutes
Prepare ahead.

Salad

2	cups rice	1	tablespoon fresh dill, chopped
3½	cups chicken broth	1	red pepper, chopped
2	tablespoons lemon juice	1	bunch scallions, chopped
1½	cups fresh parsley, chopped	1	clove garlic, minced
1	tablespoon fresh basil, chopped	½	pound feta cheese, crumbled

Dressing

¾	cup olive oil	⅓	cup red wine vinegar

- Cook rice in chicken broth and lemon juice over low heat, until liquid is absorbed. Blend in remaining salad ingredients.

- For dressing, combine oil and vinegar. Add to salad mixture and toss. Refrigerate.

Serves: 8 to 10

Refrigerator Slaw

Preparation Time: 30 minutes ~ Cook Time: 10 minutes
Prepare ahead.

1	medium cabbage, chopped finely	1	teaspoon salt
2	medium onions, sliced thinly	¾	cup light oil
⅞	cup + 2 teaspoons sugar, divided use	1	teaspoon celery seed
1	cup vinegar		

- Arrange cabbage and onions in a large glass jar by layers until all are used. Top with ⅞ cup sugar.

- Combine vinegar, 2 teaspoons sugar, salt, oil, and celery and bring to a boil. Pour over cabbage and onion mixture. Cool, cover, and refrigerate. Allow to age 3 days, stirring occasionally.

Serves: 6 to 8

Garlic Salad Dressing

Preparation Time: 10 minutes

---

3   large cloves garlic, peeled and finely
  chopped or crushed
3   tablespoons Dijon mustard
3   tablespoons red wine vinegar

¾   teaspoon salt
¾   teaspoon pepper
½   cup plus 1 tablespoon virgin olive oil

- Dressing ingredients should be put in a bowl large enough to hold a salad.

- Whisk the ingredients briefly.

- For salad, add 1 large head of desired lettuce or greens and toss.

Yield: ¾ cup dressing

Party Rice Salad

Preparation Time: 30 minutes plus refrigeration time

Salad

2   boxes Uncle Ben's Wild Rice (Original
  Flavor)
½   cup white raisins
1   bunch green onions, chopped

2   peppers (1 red, 1 yellow), chopped fine
1   cup honey roasted peanuts
1   10-ounce package frozen peas, cooked
  according to package directions

Dressing

1   teaspoon curry
¼   cup white wine vinegar

¼   cup honey
½   cup vegetable oil

- Cook rice according to directions. While rice is cooking, mix together dressing ingredients.

- When rice is done and still hot, add raisins and pour dressing over mixture. Mix well, then add remaining vegetables, except peas and nuts. Refrigerate to cool a bit, and add peas.

- Just before serving, add nuts.

Serves: 8 to 10

Parisian Marinated Salad

Preparation Time: 30 minutes plus 2 hours in the refrigerator

---

Salad

2	cups fresh mushrooms, sliced
2	9-ounce packages frozen asparagus, cooked and cut into bite sized pieces
2	14-ounce cans artichoke hearts, drained and quartered

½	cup green olives, sliced
½	cup black olives, sliced
1	small red onion, thinly sliced
2	heads red leaf lettuce, washed

Marinade

1½	cups corn oil
½	cup red wine vinegar
2	tablespoons corn syrup

2	teaspoons seasoned salt
1	tablespoon dried basil
½	teaspoon seasoned pepper

- Prepare vegetables as noted above. Except for the lettuce, place vegetables in ziplock bag.

- Combine marinade ingredients. Add to bag. Marinate in refrigerator for 2 hours. Drain vegetables, saving marinade. Serve on lettuce with drizzled marinade on top.

Serves: 8

Dried herbs are three times as potent as fresh herbs, so when using fresh instead of dried, triple the amount.

Spinach Salad
with Poppy Seed Dressing

Preparation Time: 30 minutes

Salad

1   10-ounce bag fresh spinach
1-2 oranges, sliced or 1 (11-ounce) can
    Mandarin oranges

½   cup sliced mushrooms
½   red onion, sliced in rings
¼   cup pecan halves, toasted

Dressing

½   cup sugar
2   teaspoons dry mustard
2   teaspoons salt
⅔   cup vinegar

2   cups oil
3   teaspoons poppy seeds
1   tablespoon paprika
3   teaspoons onion, grated, optional

- Place first 4 salad ingredients in a large bowl. Sprinkle pecans over top.

- Place dressing ingredients in blender and blend on low for 30 seconds or until thoroughly mixed. Just before serving pour dressing, to taste, over salad and toss.

Serves: 8 to 10

New Potato Salad Dijon with Capers

Preparation Time: 30 minutes plus refrigeration time

2   fresh spring onions, finely chopped
1   stalk celery, finely chopped
3   tablespoons red wine vinegar
2   tablespoons Dijon mustard
2   tablespoons regular olive oil

1   tablespoon mayonnaise
    (not light, not salad dressing)
1½ pounds small red potatoes, cooked and
    quartered with skin on
1   tablespoon capers (or more if you like)
    Salt and pepper to taste

- Chop onions and celery and mix thoroughly with vinegar, Dijon mustard, olive oil, and mayonnaise. Whisk mixture until completely blended.

- Pour over cooled potatoes and toss. Add capers, salt, and pepper to taste. Fold mixture together. Allow to chill 3 to 4 hours or overnight (best) before serving.

Serves: 4

Note: You may serve this recipe warm by quartering potatoes as soon as they are done and then adding the celery, onions, and sauce. The potato skins are not as easily kept on when the recipe is served warm.

Sweet and Sour Salad Dressing

Preparation Time: 15 minutes
Refrigeration Time: 4 hours

1   cup vegetable oil (or corn oil)
½   cup white vinegar
1   tablespoon dry white wine
½   cup sugar
1   teaspoon fresh squeezed lemon juice

1   teaspoon dried mustard
1   teaspoon salt
1   teaspoon paprika
2   small spring onions, finely chopped

- Whisk each ingredient as you add them in order as listed above. Stir entire mixture well. Chill 4 to 5 hours. Whisk again just before serving.

- To serve, spoon over torn salad greens, toasted walnuts or almonds, and fresh orange slices. Mandarin oranges may be substituted.

Yield: 2 cups

Eggs, Pasta and Cheese

Effortless
to Chic

Eggs, Pasta, and Cheese

Sausage and Egg Casserole

Preparation Time: 30 minutes ~ Cook Time: 35 to 40 minutes
Prepare ahead.

---

6   slices white bread, crust removed and cubed (day-old is best)

1   pound hot or mild sausage, cooked, drained, and crumbled

1½-2 cups sharp Cheddar cheese, grated, divided use

6   eggs, lightly beaten

2   cups milk

1   teaspoon dry mustard

½   teaspoon onion powder

Salt and pepper, to taste

4   ounces sliced mushrooms, fresh or canned, optional

1   cup dry bread crumbs, optional

4   tablespoons butter, melted, optional

- Place the bread cubes in a 9 x 9-inch glass baking dish. Top with crumbled sausage and ½ cup of grated cheese.

- Mix eggs and milk with mustard, onion powder, salt, pepper, and mushrooms (if desired), and pour over sausage and cheese. Top with remaining cheese and refrigerate overnight.

- If desired, combine bread crumbs and butter and sprinkle over top before baking. Bake at 350 degrees for 35 to 40 minutes.

Serves: 6

Fruit, nut bread, juice, and coffee make this a great breakfast for overnight guests!

Light and Fluffy Egg Bake

Preparation Time: 10 minutes ~ Cook Time: 50 minutes

1½	pints cottage cheese	1	teaspoon salt
½	cup cornmeal	1	teaspoon parsley, chopped
¼	cup milk	6	eggs, beaten
2	tablespoons onion, minced	1	package brown n' serve sausage links

- Mix all ingredients, except sausage. Pour mixture into a 9 x 13-inch baking pan. Place sausage on top.
- Bake at 350 degrees for about 50 minutes. Do not overbake.

Serves: 6

Holiday Morning Casserole

Preparation Time: 30 minutes ~ Cook Time: 30 minutes
May prepare ahead.

1	pound pork sausage, cooked and drained (hot variety is good)	1¼	cups buttermilk baking mix
4	ounces mushrooms, sliced	12	eggs
½	cup scallions, sliced with tops	1	cup milk
2	medium tomatoes, chopped	1½	teaspoons salt
2	cups mozzarella cheese, grated	1½	teaspoons pepper
		½	teaspoon dried oregano

- Layer sausage, mushrooms, scallions, tomatoes, and cheese in a greased 13 x 9-inch baking dish. Beat remaining ingredients and pour over sausage layers.
- Cook, uncovered, in 350 degree oven until golden brown and set, about 30 minutes. Cut into twelve 3-inch squares. Great reheated.

Serves: 12

Overnight French Toast Casserole

Preparation Time: 20 minutes ~ Cook Time: 40 minutes
Prepare ahead and refrigerate overnight.

Bread Mixture

1	10-inch loaf French bread	1	teaspoon vanilla
6	eggs	¼	teaspoon cinnamon
2	cups half-and-half	¼	teaspoon nutmeg
1	cup milk		Dash salt
2	tablespoons sugar		

Praline Topping

1	cup butter	2	tablespoons light corn syrup
1	cup packed light brown sugar	½	teaspoon cinnamon
1	cup pecans, chopped	½	teaspoon nutmeg

- Cut French bread into 20 (1-inch) slices. Arrange slices in two rows in a 13 x 9-inch baking dish.

- Combine eggs, half-and-half, milk, sugar, vanilla, cinnamon, nutmeg, and salt in a bowl. Beat with rotary beater or whisk until blended but not bubbly. Pour over bread slices, spooning some of the mixture in between slices. Refrigerate, covered, overnight.

- Make the praline topping by combining the butter, brown sugar, pecans, corn syrup, cinnamon, and nutmeg in a bowl. Mix well. Spread over the bread.

- Bake at 350 degrees for 40 minutes or until puffed and light brown. Serve with maple syrup, honey, or orange syrup.

Serves: 8 to 10

Orange Syrup

Preparation Time: 10 minutes ~ Cook Time: 10 minutes

1	6-ounce can frozen orange juice	1	cup water
1	cup light corn syrup		

- Combine all ingredients in a medium saucepan. Bring to a boil and cook for 10 minutes. Serve hot over French toast, pancakes, or waffles.

Yield: about 2½ cups

Savory Soufflé Roll

Preparation Time: 30 minutes
Cook Time: 25 to 30 minutes

4	tablespoons butter	½	teaspoon salt
½	cup flour	⅛	teaspoon white pepper
2	cups milk, heated to lukewarm in microwave	5	eggs, separated, at room temperature
			Pinch cream of tartar

- Coat a 15 x 10½ x 1-inch jelly-roll pan with cooking spray. Line with foil and coat foil with cooking spray.

- In a small saucepan, over medium heat, melt butter, and whisk in flour. Cook for a few minutes, then whisk in milk. Stir until thickened (basic white sauce). Add seasonings.

- Remove from heat and whisk in egg yolks one at a time. Cook 1 minute. Remove from heat. Beat egg whites with cream of tartar until stiff, but not dry. Fold into first mixture, gently. Spread into jelly-roll pan. Bake 25 to 30 minutes at 400 degrees.

- While soufflé is baking, make filling (see next page). Turn soufflé onto a clean tea towel and spread with hot filling. Roll, using edges of tea towel to help roll. Gently transfer to a serving dish, seam-side down. Slice into 6 servings.

Serves: 6

Savory Filling or Seafood Filling

Savory Filling

2	tablespoons butter		1	cup ham or country ham, cooked and chopped
2	tablespoons onion, finely chopped		1	tablespoon Dijon mustard
4	large mushrooms, approximately ¼ cup, chopped		¼	teaspoon nutmeg
1	cup chopped spinach, cooked and drained		6	ounces cream cheese

- Melt butter, sauté onion, and add mushrooms. Cook over medium heat 3 minutes. Add remaining ingredients, mix, and check seasonings. Cover and keep warm until soufflé is ready.

Seafood Filling

2	tablespoons butter		2	pounds cooked shrimp, chopped or 1 pound crabmeat
2	tablespoons onion, finely chopped		2	tablespoons fresh dill, minced
4	large mushrooms, approximately ¼ cup, chopped		6	ounces cream cheese

- Melt butter, sauté onion, and add mushrooms. Cook over medium heat 3 minutes. Add remaining ingredients, mix, and check seasonings. Cover and keep warm until soufflé is ready.

Southwest Crustless Quiche

Preparation Time: 30 minutes ~ Cook Time: 45 minutes
May prepare ahead.

8	eggs	1	stick butter, melted
½	pound Cheddar cheese, grated	1	7-ounce can mild green chilies, chopped
½	pound Monterey Jack cheese, grated	½	cup all-purpose flour
1	pint cottage cheese	1	teaspoon baking powder

- Preheat oven to 350 degrees. Butter a 9 x 13-inch baking dish.

- Combine first 6 ingredients, mixing well. Combine flour and baking powder and stir into other mixture, blending well.

- Pour into prepared dish and bake until brown and set, about 45 minutes. Cut into squares.

Yield: 12 main dish servings or 24 appetizers

Emergency Artichoke Sauce

Preparation Time: 15 minutes
May prepare ahead.

¼	cup butter or margarine	2	tablespoons fresh basil or any herb, chopped
¼	cup olive oil		
4-6	garlic cloves, minced or pressed	1	tablespoon fresh lemon juice
1	14-ounce can artichoke hearts, drained and chopped		Ground black pepper and salt to taste

- Warm the butter and oil together in a non-reactive saucepan. After the butter has melted, add the garlic and sauté for about 2 minutes (until just golden).

- Add the chopped artichoke hearts, fresh herbs, lemon juice, salt, and pepper. Heat gently for about 10 minutes.

- Serve warm over pasta with a sprinkling of Parmesan cheese or spoon over broiled fish or baked potatoes. If reheating, warm gently.

Yield: 1½ cups

Italian Spinach Pie

Preparation Time: 20 minutes ~ Cook Time: 55 minutes

2   10-ounce packages frozen chopped
     spinach
½   cup onion, finely chopped
2   large cloves garlic, finely chopped
⅓   cup olive oil

½   pound sharp Cheddar cheese, grated
5   eggs, beaten
     Salt and pepper to taste
1   refrigerator pie crust

• Cook spinach and drain thoroughly, squeeze out very well. Sauté onion and garlic in olive oil. Mix together all ingredients except pie crust.

• Pour into pie crust. Bake at 425 degrees for 15 minutes, reduce oven to 325 degrees and bake for 40 minutes.

Serves: 6

Chilled Seafood Delight

Preparation Time: 40 minutes
Prepare ahead.

4½   cups water
1½   pounds unpeeled medium shrimp
1   16-ounce package linguine
1   6-ounce package frozen snow peas,
     thawed and drained
6   green onions, chopped
4   medium tomatoes, peeled and chopped

¾   cup olive oil
¼   cup fresh parsley, chopped
⅓   cup white wine vinegar
1   teaspoon dried whole oregano
1½   teaspoons dried whole basil
½   teaspoon garlic salt
½   teaspoon ground black pepper

• Boil shrimp in water for 3 to 4 minutes. Drain well. Rinse in cold water. Chill, peel, and devein.

• Cook linguine, omitting the salt. Rinse with cold water and drain.

• Combine shrimp, linguine, and all other ingredients. Toss gently, cover, and chill at least 2 hours. (Longer is better.)

Serves: 10

Mushroom Pasta Torte

Preparation Time: 30 minutes ~ Cook Time: 45 minutes
May prepare ahead.

2	tablespoons butter	1	tablespoon all-purpose flour
1	pound fresh mushrooms, thinly sliced	⅔	cup heavy cream
1	cup sweet onion, slivered or sliced thinly	½	cup sour cream
½	teaspoon salt	1	cup each of Cheddar and Monterey Jack cheese, grated, plus optional ½ cup extra for topping
¼	teaspoon white pepper		
½	cup white wine (such as Chardonnay or sauterne)	2	eggs, beaten
1	cup angel hair pasta, raw and chopped	1	unbaked pie shell for 9 or 10-inch round pan

- Melt butter in large sauté pan. Add mushrooms, onions, salt, pepper, and wine. Cook on low heat approximately 15 minutes until 2 to 3 tablespoons of liquid remain. Prepare pasta as directed while cooking mushrooms and onion.

- When mushroom mixture has 2 to 3 tablespoons of liquid remaining, stir in flour, followed by ⅔ cup heavy cream. Increase heat to medium and stir constantly for 3 to 4 minutes until mixture thickens, but is not dry.

- Remove from heat. Stir in sour cream, cheeses, pasta, and eggs. Fold into pie shell. Bake 45 minutes at 350 degrees. Remove from oven to sprinkle ½ cup grated cheese on top, if desired. Return to oven just until cheese melts. Serve warm.

Serves: 8

Spaghetti Sauce with a Punch

Preparation Time: 30 minutes ~ Cook Time: minimum 3 hours
Prepare ahead.

1½	pounds lean (80%) ground beef	2	tablespoons chili powder
1	large onion, chopped	1	tablespoon oregano
2	teaspoons garlic, minced	1	6-ounce can tomato paste
1	green pepper, chopped	1	29-ounce can tomato puree
2	stalks celery, chopped	1	8-ounce can tomato sauce
2-3	bay leaves		A few fresh mushrooms, sliced
½	tablespoon crushed red pepper flakes		

- Cook beef and onion in a large heavy pot until beef is no longer red and break up meat. Add the remaining ingredients and stir. Cook over low heat. Cover. Stir frequently. Simmer for several hours (about 3 hours minimum.)

- Serve over cooked spaghetti. Add a sprinkling of Parmesan or Romano cheese if desired.

Serves: 6 to 8

Every summer our family of five children would travel many hours to spend one glorious week at the seashore. Late Saturday afternoon, after our very long journey, we would rush to the ocean for an hour or two before dinner. Every year my mother would have a big pot of spaghetti sauce and mounds of spaghetti waiting for us on our return. Warm, spicy red sauce and meatballs would fill our ravenous appetites. Saturday night spaghetti and meatballs is a ritual!

Special Spaghetti Casserole

Preparation Time: 30 minutes ~ Cook Time: 30 minutes
May prepare ahead.

1½ tablespoons oil	7 ounces spaghetti, uncooked
1 pound ground beef	4 ounces cream cheese
1 medium onion, chopped	1 cup cottage cheese
1 4-ounce jar mushrooms	¼ cup chives, chopped
1 8-ounce can tomato sauce	¼ cup sour cream
1 6-ounce can tomato paste	2 tablespoons butter, melted
1 teaspoon oregano	¼ cup bread crumbs
1 teaspoon garlic powder	Parmesan cheese, grated

- Sauté beef and onions in oil. Drain. Combine next 5 ingredients with meat mixture. Simmer uncovered for 15 minutes.

- Meanwhile, cook the spaghetti. Drain.

- Place half of the cooked spaghetti in a 9 x 9-inch casserole. Combine cream cheese and cottage cheese, chives, and sour cream. Mix well. Spoon evenly over spaghetti.

- Place remainder of spaghetti on top of cheese mixture. Pour meat mixture over top layer of spaghetti. Combine bread crumbs with melted butter. Sprinkle with bread crumbs and Parmesan cheese. Bake at 350 degrees for 30 minutes.

Serves: 6

Spicy Red Pepper Capellini

Preparation Time: 20 minutes ~ Cook Time: 50 minutes

4	red bell peppers		2	cups chicken stock, canned broth is fine
1	pound onions		1	pound capellini or angel hair pasta
4	tablespoons extra virgin olive oil			Salt to taste
2	large, fresh garlic cloves, peeled and finely chopped or pressed		¾	cup fresh Parmesan cheese (3 ounces), grated
½	teaspoon crushed red pepper flakes, or to taste			

- Halve the peppers, clean out seeds and veins. Chop and set aside. Slice the onions in half lengthwise. Cut crosswise into very thin slices. Set aside.

- In a large skillet, heat the oil over moderate heat until hot, but not smoking. Add the peppers, lightly salt, and cook until softened, stirring, about 5 minutes. Add the onions, garlic, and red pepper flakes. (Do not let the onions brown.) Cook about 10 minutes. Add the stock and simmer over moderate heat, uncovered, about 30 minutes.

- Transfer the mixture in small batches to a blender or food processor. Process to a coarse puree. Return to the skillet and reheat over low heat.

- Cook capellini in 6 quarts boiling water with 2 tablespoons salt, (approximately 2½ to 3 minutes). Drain.

- Place drained pasta in a large bowl and add about ½ the cheese. Toss thoroughly until the cheese has been absorbed. Add the sauce and toss again, until the sauce is absorbed. Serve in large shallow bowls. Top with the remaining cheese.

Serves: 4 to 6

Spinach-Spaghetti Bake

Preparation Time: 30 minutes ~ Cook Time: 45 minutes
May prepare ahead.

---

9 ounces spaghetti, broken into pieces, cooked al dente, and drained
1 stick butter, melted
2 10-ounce packages frozen chopped spinach, cooked and drained
2 cups Monterey Jack cheese, grated
2 cups mozzarella, grated
¼ pound mushrooms, sliced

2 cups sour cream (may use reduced-fat sour cream)
¼ cup onion, minced
½ teaspoon salt
¼ teaspoon fresh ground pepper
¼ teaspoon oregano, dried or ¾ teaspoon fresh oregano

- While heating the water for the spaghetti, and cooking the spaghetti, microwave the spinach. Drain the spaghetti and press the excess water out of the spinach.

- Stir together all ingredients. Place into a 9 x 13-inch casserole dish prepared with cooking spray. Bake, uncovered, at 350 degrees for 45 minutes.

Serves: 8 to 10

Vegetable Lasagna

Preparation Time: 15 minutes ~ Cook Time: 1 hour and 15 minutes

---

1 10-ounce package frozen chopped spinach
1½ cups mozzarella cheese, grated, divided use
1 egg, beaten
16 ounces ricotta cheese
1 teaspoon salt

⅛ teaspoon pepper
¾ teaspoon oregano
1 32-ounce jar spaghetti sauce
8 ounces lasagna, uncooked
1 cup water

- Thaw and drain spinach. Combine 1 cup mozzarella cheese, egg, ricotta cheese, salt, pepper, oregano, and spinach and mix well.

- Spray a 9 x 13-inch pan with cooking spray. Spread ½ cup spaghetti sauce on bottom of pan. Layer one half of the lasagna, then one half of the spinach mixture, and ½ cup of spaghetti sauce. Repeat layers and top with remaining mozzarella.

- Carefully pour 1 cup of water around the inside edge of baking dish. Cover tightly with aluminum foil and bake at 350 degrees for 75 minutes. Let cool about 10 minutes before serving.

Serves: 4 to 6

Summer Pasta

Preparation Time: 30 minutes ~ Cook Time: total about 20 minutes

1	pound shrimp, peeled and deveined
	Wooden skewers
	Olive oil
	Cajun seafood spice
	Lemons
1	pound spaghetti
½	pound asparagus, sliced diagonally into 1-inch pieces

1	large bunch green onions, sliced (use all the white and as much of the green as looks tender and light green)
2	cups very fresh corn, cut from the cob
2	large tomatoes, chopped, save accumulated juices

- Put shrimp on skewers so they can be easily turned. Brush with olive oil and season heavily with Cajun spice. Broil until just done, 1½ to 2 minutes on each side. When you turn them, squeeze half a lemon over them. Remove and set aside when done.

- Cook spaghetti in salted water until tender. (Break it in half first, because it is easier to mix with other ingredients.) Drain.

- Cook asparagus in boiling, salted water 3 or 4 minutes, until barely tender. Drain.

- While spaghetti is cooking, sauté green onion and corn in several tablespoons olive oil, just until corn is tender. (This will only take a couple of minutes.) Mix in tomato with any accumulated juice, and cooked asparagus, and remove from heat.

- Season to taste with salt and ground pepper. Mix well with the drained spaghetti. Remove shrimp from skewers and arrange on top, or mix in, as you prefer.

Serves: 4

Serve with a loaf of bread and a bottle of wine and you have a very pretty and delicious one-dish meal!

Spicy Cheese
Artichoke Gratin

Preparation Time: 15 minutes ~ Cook Time: 30 to 40 minutes

¾ cup picante sauce
   (hot, medium, or mild, to taste)

1 cup artichoke hearts, chopped
   (frozen or canned)

¼ cup Parmesan cheese, grated

1 cup Monterey Jack cheese, grated

1 cup sharp Cheddar cheese, grated

6 large eggs

1 8-ounce container sour cream
   Parsley sprigs for garnish, if desired

- Butter a 10-inch quiche dish. Spread the picante sauce on the bottom. Distribute the chopped artichokes evenly over the picante sauce.

- Sprinkle Parmesan cheese over the artichokes. Sprinkle with Monterey Jack cheese and Cheddar cheese.

- Blend the eggs in a blender until mixture is smooth. Add the sour cream to the eggs and blend until mixed. Pour the egg mixture over the cheeses.

- Bake, uncovered, at 350 degrees for 30 to 40 minutes or until set. Cut into wedges and serve garnished with parsley.

Serves: 6

Easy Cheese Timbale

Preparation Time: 15 minutes ~ Cook Time: 45 minutes
Prepare ahead.

3-4 tablespoons butter, softened
8 slices white bread
8 ounces sharp Cheddar cheese, grated
2½ cups milk

4 eggs
1 teaspoon dry mustard
1 teaspoon salt

- Butter bread, remove crusts, and cut into fourths. Place half the bread slices in a 2-quart soufflé dish. Cover with half the cheese. Repeat layers.
- Beat remaining ingredients together and pour over the bread and cheese. Let sit in refrigerator, covered, for 12 to 24 hours.
- Bake, uncovered, at 350 degrees for 45 minutes or until brown and firm. Bakes better if you place the soufflé dish in a larger baking dish containing an inch or two of water.

Serves: 8

Fresh Tomato Pie

Preparation Time: 15 minutes ~ Cook Time: 45 minutes

3 eggs
¼ cup milk
Salt and pepper to taste
2 medium ripe tomatoes, sliced

1 medium sweet onion, sliced thinly
1 cup Cheddar cheese (medium-sharp), grated
1 deep-dish pie crust

- Beat eggs, milk, salt, and pepper until well mixed.
- Layer tomatoes, onions, and cheese in unbaked pie crust. Pour egg mixture on top.
- Bake at 375 degrees for 45 minutes. This freezes well after baking.

Serves: 6

Tomato Eggplant Tart

Preparation Time: 30 to 40 minutes ~ Cook Time: 45 to 50 minutes
May prepare ahead.

1 17. 3-ounce package frozen puff pastry, thawed (2 sheets)
1 medium eggplant, thinly sliced
2 tablespoons olive oil
2 cloves garlic, crushed
2 teaspoons salt
1 teaspoon pepper
3 cups mozzarella cheese, grated, divided use
1 cup mayonnaise
2 cups fresh basil leaves, torn
10 Roma tomatoes, chopped and drained
1 tablespoon all-purpose flour
1 egg, beaten
   Fresh basil leaves and a dollop of sour cream for garnish, optional

- Line a 10-inch springform pan with puff pastry. Seal any seams or tears with drops of water. Bake 20 minutes at 375 degrees while preparing other ingredients. Set aside to cool.

- Sear eggplant in olive oil and garlic on high heat until slightly browned. Remove from heat, add salt and pepper. Drain on paper towel. Sprinkle ½ cup mozzarella in bottom of puff pastry.

- Combine remaining mozzarella with mayonnaise, basil, tomatoes, flour, and egg.

- Layer ½ eggplant in pastry. Top with ½ cheese-tomato-basil mixture. Arrange second layer of eggplant slices followed by remaining cheese-tomato-basil mixture.

- Bake at 375 degrees for 45 to 50 minutes. Excellent served warm, but also good at room temperature.

Serves: 10 to 12

Zucchini Crescent Pie

Preparation Time: 30 minutes ~ Cook Time: 20 minutes

1 cup onion, chopped	½ teaspoon pepper
4 cups unpeeled zucchini, sliced	¼ teaspoon oregano
⅓ cup butter	2 eggs, beaten
½ cup fresh parsley, chopped or 2 tablespoons flakes	8 ounces mozzarella or Muenster cheese, grated (2 cups)
½ teaspoon garlic powder	2 teaspoons Dijon mustard
½ teaspoon basil leaves	1 8-ounce can crescent rolls
½ teaspoon salt	

- Cook onion and squash in butter until tender (10 minutes). Stir in seasonings. Remove from heat. Blend eggs and cheese. Stir into squash.

- Line pie plate or casserole dish with crescent roll triangles, spread with mustard, pour in mixture.

- Bake at 375 degrees for 18 to 20 minutes until crust is lightly browned. Let stand 10 minutes before serving.

Serves: 6

Two-Cheese Grits

Preparation Time: 30 minutes ~ Cook Time: 45 minutes

2½ cups sour cream	¾ pound Monterey Jack cheese, cut into strips
3 green jalapeños, seeded and finely chopped (optional, or may use 1 4-ounce can mild green chilies)	Salt and pepper, to taste
3 cups cooked grits	¾ cup Cheddar cheese, grated

- Mix sour cream and jalapeños. Butter a 1½-quart casserole.

- Place ⅓ of grits in casserole, then half the sour cream mixture, then half the Monterey Jack cheese strips. Repeat layers ending with a layer of grits. Season with salt and pepper.

- Bake at 350 degrees for 30 minutes. Sprinkle with Cheddar cheese during the last few minutes of baking and allow to melt and bubble before serving.

Serves: 4 to 6

Cheese Pie

Preparation Time: 20 minutes ~ Cook Time: 60 minutes

2	refrigerator pie crusts	4	eggs, divided use
2	cans French fried onions	2	cups milk, divided use
2	cups Cheddar cheese, grated	¼	teaspoon pepper, divided use

- Place pie crusts in 9-inch pie pans, prick, and bake at 425 degrees for 7 minutes. Remove from oven. Reduce oven to 350 degrees.

- In each pie shell sprinkle 1 can fried onions and 1 cup Cheddar cheese. Beat together 2 eggs, 1 cup milk, and ⅛ teaspoon pepper and pour into one pie shell over onions and cheese. Repeat for second pie shell.

- Bake at 350 degrees for 60 minutes. Cool 5 minutes before serving.

Serves: 16

Variation: Use 2 deep-dish pie shells and add 1 (10-ounce) package frozen broccoli, 6 ounces chopped ham, and 1 (15-ounce) can mushrooms divided between 2 pie shells in addition to French fried onions and cheese. Increase to 5 eggs and 2½ cups milk. Bake until toothpick inserted comes out clean and pie is set.

Chile Cheese Brunch Dish

Preparation Time: 10 minutes ~ Cook Time: 45 minutes

3	eggs	1	cup flour
3	cups milk	1	teaspoon baking powder
2	4-ounce cans mild green chilies, chopped (may use half mild chilies and half jalapeños, if more spice is desired)	1	pound Cheddar cheese, grated
		1	teaspoon salt

- Beat eggs and add milk. Put chilies, flour, baking powder, cheese, and salt in a bowl.

- Add milk mixture and stir gently. Pour into a buttered 9 x 12-inch baking dish. Bake at 350 degrees for 45 minutes.

Serves: 8

Breads, Sandwiches, and Soups

Basic to Sumptuous

Breads, Sandwiches, and Soups

Angel Biscuits

Preparation Time: 30 minutes ~ Cook Time: 12 to 15 minutes

1	package dry yeast	¼	cup sugar
2	tablespoons warm water (105 to 115 degrees)	1	tablespoon baking powder
		1	teaspoon baking soda
2	cups buttermilk	1	teaspoon salt
5	cups all-purpose flour	1	cup vegetable shortening

- Combine yeast in warm water. Let stand 5 minutes until bubbly. Add buttermilk to yeast mixture and set aside.

- Combine dry ingredients in a large bowl, cut in shortening with a pastry blender until mixture looks like coarse crumbs. Add buttermilk mixture and mix with a fork until ingredients are moistened.

- Turn dough onto a floured surface and knead 3 or 4 times. Roll dough to ½-inch thickness.

- Cut into biscuits and place on lightly greased baking sheet. Bake at 400 degrees for 12 to 15 minutes.

Yield: 2 to 3 dozen

When we were small children, we used to visit our grandparents in the North Carolina mountains. Every morning the house would be filled with the smells of breakfast cooking- bacon, eggs, warm apples, and, best of all, my grandmother's "baby" biscuits. Before baking the biscuits, my grandmother would roll out the dough and let each of the grand- children cut out some biscuits with a miniature biscuit cutter. It was metal with a red painted knob on top. Our "baby" biscuits tasted better than anything we could imagine, especially with the homemade apple butter my grandfather made! We'll never forget those cool summer mornings in the mountains with my grandparents, especially the smells and tastes of breakfast and our yummy "baby" biscuits!

Cheese Buttons

Preparation Time: 45 minutes ~ Cook Time: 12 to 15 minutes
May prepare ahead. Freezes well.

½ cup butter or margarine, softened
1 cup all-purpose flour
1 cup sharp Cheddar cheese, shredded and softened
½ teaspoon salt

Dash cayenne pepper or a few drops of hot pepper sauce, to taste
1 cup crispy rice cereal
Paprika, optional

- Mix butter, cheese, flour, salt, and pepper in large bowl by hand until well blended. Briefly work in the cereal. Do not overwork. Chill dough about 15 minutes.

- When ready to bake, roll into small balls about the size of a quarter and place 1½ inches apart on ungreased cookie sheet. Flatten each ball with a fork to make a criss-cross pattern. Bake at 350 degrees for 12 to 15 minutes until lightly brown.

- Sprinkle with paprika. Cool on wire rack. Store in airtight container for up to 2 weeks. This recipe can be doubled.

Yield: 3 dozen

Variation: Top with a pecan half.

Mini Cheese Muffins

Preparation Time: 10 minutes ~ Cook Time: 10 minutes

2 cups baking mix
1 cup sour cream

1½ cups sharp Cheddar cheese, grated
1 stick butter, melted

- Combine all ingredients and mix well into a sticky paste. Drop by spoonfuls into mini muffin tins, either well-greased or nonstick.

- Bake at 450 degrees for 10 minutes or until slightly brown on top. May be frozen. To reheat, thaw and place on cookie sheet in 350 degree oven until warm.

Yield: 36 mini muffins

Variations: May add ham bits, jalapeño peppers, crumbled sausage, etc. to vary flavor of muffins.

Blueberry Muffins

Preparation Time: 10 minutes ~ Cook Time: 20 minutes

1½ cups flour
½   teaspoon baking soda
½   teaspoon salt
1½ teaspoons baking powder
1¼ cups brown sugar

½   cup butter, melted
2   eggs
½   cup milk
1   cup fresh or frozen blueberries
¼   cup flour

- Grease muffin tins.

- Sift first 4 ingredients into large bowl. Add brown sugar, melted butter, eggs, and milk, and stir. If batter is a bit lumpy, then it is perfect.

- Lightly flour berries with remaining ¼ cup flour and fold into batter. Fill muffin tins ½ full. Bake at 375 degrees for 20 minutes. Remove from muffin pans while warm.

Yield: 1½ dozen

Refrigerator Bran Muffins

Preparation Time: 30 minutes ~ Cook Time: 15 to 20 minutes
May prepare ahead.

1   cup 100% Bran cereal
1   cup boiling water
⅔   cup shortening
1½ cups sugar
2   eggs, beaten

2   cups buttermilk
2½ cups flour
2½ teaspoons baking soda
½   teaspoon salt
2   cups All-Bran cereal

- Pour boiling water over 100% Bran cereal. Cool.

- Cream together shortening and sugar. Add eggs and buttermilk. Add bran.

- Sift together flour, soda, and salt. Add to mixture. Fold in All-Bran.

- Bake in greased muffin tins at 400 degrees for 15 to 20 minutes. Batter keeps in refrigerator 4 weeks.

Yield: 3 dozen

Crumb Cake Muffins

Preparation Time: 20 minutes ~ Cook Time: 12 to 14 minutes

Topping

½	cup flour	2	teaspoons cinnamon
⅓	cup sugar	4	tablespoons butter, cut into small pieces

Batter

1	cup flour	⅛	teaspoon nutmeg
⅔	cup sugar	¼	cup buttermilk
¼	teaspoon baking powder	2	tablespoons butter, melted
¼	teaspoon baking soda	1	egg
⅛	teaspoon salt	¼	teaspoon vanilla

- Grease a 12-muffin tin.

- For topping, combine flour, sugar, and cinnamon. Cut butter into mixture until it resembles coarse crumbs. Place topping in refrigerator while the batter is being made.

- For batter, use medium-sized bowl and whisk together flour, sugar, baking powder, baking soda, salt, and nutmeg.

- In small bowl, combine buttermilk, butter, egg, and vanilla. Pour buttermilk mixture into flour mixture, whisking until smooth.

- Evenly divide batter among muffin cups. Sprinkle topping over batter, and pat down gently. Bake at 375 degrees for 12 to 14 minutes.

Yield: 12 muffins

For lighter muffins, place greased muffin tins in the oven for a few moments before adding the batter.

If your muffin batter is full of lumps, then it is perfect.

Sweet Potato Muffins

Preparation: 10 minutes ~ Cook Time: 25 minutes

½ cup butter
1¼ cups sugar
2 eggs
1¼ cups sweet potatoes, cooked and mashed (baked sweet potatoes, not boiled or canned)
1½ cups all-purpose flour

2 teaspoons baking powder
¼ teaspoon salt
1 teaspoon cinnamon
¼ teaspoon nutmeg
1 cup milk
¼ cup chopped nuts, optional
¼ cup raisins, optional

- Preheat oven to 400 degrees.

- Cream together butter and sugar. Add eggs. Blend in sweet potatoes.

- Sift dry ingredients and add alternately with milk. If desired, fold in nuts and/or raisins.

- Spoon into muffin pan coated with cooking spray. Bake 25 minutes. May also be prepared in mini muffin pans.

Yield: 12 regular size muffins or 2 dozen mini muffins

Black~Eyed Pea Cornbread

Preparation Time: 15 minutes ~ Cook Time: 40 minutes
May prepare ahead.

---

1 pound hot sausage
1 medium onion, chopped
2 eggs
1½ cups self-rising cornmeal

1 cup milk
1 15.5-ounce can black-eyed peas, drained
2 cups sharp Cheddar cheese, grated
¾ cup cream-style corn

- Cook sausage and onion until browned. Drain off fat.

- Add all other ingredients and mix well.

- Pour into a 13 x 9-inch pan that has been coated with cooking spray. Bake at 350 degrees for about 40 minutes, until a toothpick inserted into center comes out clean.

Serves: 8 to 10

Broccoli Cornbread

Preparation Time: 15 minutes ~ Cook Time: 30 to 40 minutes

4	eggs	1	cup cottage cheese
1	10-ounce package frozen chopped broccoli, thawed	1	small onion, chopped
			Dash salt
6	tablespoons butter or margarine, melted	1	6 to 7.5-ounce package corn muffin mix

- Beat eggs in medium bowl, then add all other ingredients. Mix well and pour into a 9 x 9-inch baking dish that has been sprayed with cooking spray.

- Bake at 400 degrees for 20 to 30 minutes or until browned on top. Serve on plate like spoonbread.

Serves: 8

Cheese Spoonbread

Preparation Time: 30 minutes ~ Cook Time: 30 minutes

2	cups milk	6	ounces Cheddar cheese, grated
1	scant cup cornmeal	2	teaspoons baking powder
½	teaspoon salt	4	eggs, separated, at room temperature
2	tablespoons sugar	1	cup country ham, minced, optional
1	tablespoon butter		Pinch cream of tartar

- Butter a 1½-quart soufflé dish or deep casserole dish.

- Scald milk in a small saucepan. Whisk in cornmeal, a little at a time. Whisk 2 minutes over low heat.

- Whisk in salt, sugar, and butter. Add cheese and mix thoroughly. Remove from heat and let cool.

- Sprinkle baking powder over mixture and incorporate. Beat in egg yolks. Stir in country ham, if desired.

- In a separate bowl, whip egg whites with cream of tartar to soft peaks. Fold egg whites and cornmeal mixture together.

- Pour into soufflé dish and bake 30 minutes at 350 degrees.

Serves: 4 as a brunch dish or 6 as a side dish

Sour Cream Waffles

Preparation Time: 30 to 45 minutes

2	eggs, separated
⅓	cup sugar
2	tablespoons butter, melted
1	cup sour cream
1	cup flour

¼	teaspoon salt
¼	teaspoon baking powder
¾	teaspoon baking soda
	Milk

- Beat egg whites until fluffy and set aside.

- Heat waffle iron. Beat egg yolks, sugar, and melted butter until light and fluffy. Add sour cream, flour, salt, baking powder, and sugar.

- Dissolve baking soda in a little milk. Add to mixture. Fold in fluffy beaten egg whites. Batter should have consistency of whipped cream.

- Cook in preheated waffle iron.

Yield: 4 to 6 waffles

A bit of sugar in pancake or waffle batter will make them brown more quickly.

Basic Pancakes

Preparation Time: 10 minutes

1¼	cups flour
2½	teaspoons baking powder
2	tablespoons sugar
¾	teaspoon salt

1	egg
1¼	cups milk
3	tablespoons salad oil

- Mix slightly, leave lumpy.

- Pour small amounts on medium griddle. Turn when covered with bubbles.

Yield: 20 (4-inch) pancakes

Cinnamon Swirl Coffee Cake

Preparation Time: 30 minutes ~ Cook Time: 50 to 55 minutes

Batter

2	sticks unsalted butter, softened		½	teaspoon baking powder
1	cup sugar		½	teaspoon baking soda
2	teaspoons vanilla extract			Pinch salt
3	large eggs, at room temperature		½	cup sour cream
2	cups all-purpose flour			

Syrup

2	tablespoons unsalted butter, melted		1	teaspoon ground cinnamon
3	teaspoons sugar			

Streusel

1	cup firmly packed light brown sugar		1	stick cold unsalted butter, cut into tablespoons
2	teaspoons ground cinnamon			
1	cup pecans, toasted and chopped			

- Butter and flour a 10-inch tube pan, and use parchment paper for easy removal.

- For the batter, cream butter and sugar in a bowl with electric mixer on medium speed until fluffy, about 5 minutes. Scrape down the bowl. Add the vanilla and eggs, 1 at a time, beating for 20 seconds after each addition. Scrape down the bowl again.

- In another bowl, whisk together the flour, baking powder, baking soda, and salt. Add this mixture to the butter mixture in thirds, alternating with the sour cream. Beat for 45 seconds after each addition, and begin and end with the flour mixture. Pour the batter into the prepared tube pan.

- For the syrup, stir together melted butter, sugar, and cinnamon in a small bowl.

- Drizzle the syrup over the batter and with the blade of a knife, or a skewer, swirl the syrup through the batter.

- For the streusel, combine the sugar, cinnamon, and pecans in a bowl. With a pastry cutter, cut in the butter, a few pieces at a time, until the mixture resembles coarse crumbs. Scatter the streusel over the batter in the pan.

- Bake at 350 degrees for 50 to 55 minutes, or until a cake tester into the center comes out clean. Remove the pan from the oven to a wire rack to cool for 15 minutes. Serve warm or at room temperature.

Serves: 12

Father James' Blueberry Coffee Cake

Preparation Time: 20 minutes ~ Cook Time: 45 minutes

Batter

2	cups sugar	½	teaspoon salt
½	cup butter (do not use margarine)	1	teaspoon vanilla
2	eggs	½	cup milk
1	teaspoon fresh lemon rind, grated	2	cups blueberries
2	cups flour, divided use		
2	teaspoons baking powder		

Topping

½	cup sugar	¼	cup cold butter
⅓	cup flour	½	cup nuts, chopped
1	teaspoon cinnamon		

- For batter, cream butter and sugar until fluffy. Add eggs and lemon rind.

- Sift flour (reserving 1 teaspoon for blueberries), baking powder, and salt. Add dry ingredients to butter and sugar. Add vanilla and milk.

- Sprinkle berries with remaining 1 teaspoon flour and fold into batter. Pour into a 10-inch Bundt pan that has been buttered and floured.

- For topping, crumble together sugar, flour, cinnamon, butter, and nuts until well mixed. Sprinkle onto cake batter.

- Bake for 45 minutes at 375 degrees.

Serves: 10

Carrot-Apple Bread

Preparation Time: 30 minutes ~ Cook Time: 1 hour

3	cups all-purpose flour	3	eggs, beaten
¾	teaspoon salt	1	cup vegetable oil
1	teaspoon baking soda	1	cup carrots, grated
2	cups sugar	1	cup apple, pared, cored, and grated
1	teaspoon ground cinnamon	1	8-ounce can crushed pineapple, drained
1	cup pecans or walnuts, chopped	2	teaspoons vanilla extract

- Combine first 5 ingredients. Stir in pecans.
- Combine remaining ingredients and add to flour mixture, stirring just until dry ingredients are moistened.
- Spoon batter into 2 greased and floured 9 x 5-inch loaf pans. Bake at 350 degrees for 60 minutes or until a wooden pick inserted in center comes out clean.
- Cool in pans 10 minutes. Remove from pans and cool on wire racks.

Yield: 2 loaves

It's Great Banana Bread

Preparation Time: 10 minutes ~ Cook Time: 1 hour

3	cups flour	1½	teaspoons vanilla
2	cups sugar	1	8-ounce can crushed pineapple with juice
½	teaspoon salt	1½	cups vegetable oil
1	teaspoon baking soda	3	eggs, slightly beaten
1½	teaspoons cinnamon	2	cups mashed bananas

- Grease and flour 2 loaf pans. Sift together dry ingredients. Mix with remaining ingredients until "wet".
- Pour batter into prepared loaf pans. Bake at 350 degrees for 1 hour.

Yield: 2 loaves

This makes the best banana bread we've ever eaten!

Cran-Orange Nut Bread

Preparation Time: 20 minutes ~ Cook Time: 55 to 65 minutes

2 cups all-purpose flour	1 tablespoon orange peel, grated
¾ cup sugar	¾ cup orange juice
1½ teaspoons baking powder	1 egg
¾ teaspoon salt	1 cup cranberries, coarsely chopped
½ teaspoon baking soda	½ cup nuts, chopped
¼ cup butter, softened	

- Grease loaf pan. Mix flour, sugar, baking powder, salt, and baking soda. Stir in butter until mix is crumbly. Add orange peel, juice, and egg until moistened. Do not over-mix. Stir in cranberries and nuts.

- Pour into pan. Bake until wooden pick inserted into center of loaf comes out clean, about 55 to 65 minutes.

- Loosen sides of loaf from pan. Remove from pan and cool completely before slicing or freezing. This makes a festive Christmas gift when given with a jar of port wine jelly!

Serves: 8 to 10

Port Wine Jelly

3 cups port wine	4 cups sugar
1 box Sure Jell or 1 package of liquid pectin	

- Bring wine and Sure Jell to a full boil. Add sugar all at once and stir constantly, while returning to a boil. Boil for 1 minute continuing to stir. Remove from heat and pour into sterilized jars (½ pint) or other containers. Seal immediately or pour hot paraffin to ¼-inch thickness to seal.

Lemon Bread

Preparation Time: 20 minutes ~ Cook Time: 45 minutes

Bread

⅓ cup butter, melted

1 cup sugar

3 teaspoons lemon extract

2 eggs

1½ cups flour

1 teaspoon salt

1 teaspoon baking powder

½ cup milk

1 tablespoon plus 2 teaspoons fresh lemon zest, grated

½ cup pecans, chopped

Lemon Glaze

¼ cup fresh lemon juice

½ cup sugar

- Cream butter, sugar, and lemon extract. Add eggs. Combine flour, salt, and baking powder. Add ⅓ of dry ingredients at a time to butter mixture, alternating with the milk. Do not over-mix.

- Fold in lemon zest and nuts. Pour into a buttered loaf pan and bake at 350 degrees about 45 minutes or until done.

- While bread is baking make glaze by heating lemon juice and sugar until sugar dissolves. Remove loaf from oven, pour glaze slowly over top. Let stand on rack for 15 to 20 minutes, then remove loaf from pan to finish cooling.

Yield: 1 loaf

Poppy Seed Bread

Preparation Time: 15 minutes
Cook Time: 30 to 60 minutes, depending on pan size

Bread

1	package butter cake mix	¼	cup poppy seeds
1	cup hot tap water	1	cup pecans, chopped
½	cup vegetable oil	4	eggs
1	3-ounce package instant coconut cream pudding		

Glaze

1½	cups powdered sugar	¼	teaspoon butter flavor
2	tablespoons orange juice	¼	teaspoon almond flavor
¼	teaspoon vanilla		

- Spray Bundt pan with cooking spray or may use 6 small loaf pans.

- Mix all ingredients together and pour into pan. Bake at 350 degrees for 30 minutes for small loaf pans or 60 minutes for Bundt pan.

- While still warm, mix glaze ingredients together and dribble over cake.

Yield: 10 to 12 servings or 6 small loaves

Buttered Beer Bread

Preparation Time: 15 minutes ~ Bake Time: 40 minutes

6	cups self-rising flour	2	12-ounce cans cold beer
6	tablespoons sugar	1	cup butter, melted

- Combine flour, sugar, and beer. Mix well.

- Pour into 2 buttered 9 x 5-inch loaf pans. Bake at 350 degrees for 30 minutes. Pour butter over top and cook 10 additional minutes or until lightly browned. Serve warm.

Yield: 2 loaves

Pumpkin Bread Deluxe

Preparation Time: 30 minutes ~ Cook Time: 60 minutes
May prepare ahead.

1 cup butter, softened	1 teaspoon ground cloves
3 cups sugar	½ teaspoon ground nutmeg
3 large eggs	1 16-ounce can pumpkin
3 cups all-purpose flour	(not pumpkin pie mix)
1 teaspoon baking soda	1 teaspoon vanilla extract
1 teaspoon baking powder	1 cup pecans or walnuts, chopped
1 teaspoon salt	(or may use raisins)
1 teaspoon ground cinnamon	

- Butter and flour 2 (9 x 5-inch) loaf pans or 6 mini-loaf pans.

- Cream butter and sugar at medium speed of electric mixer. Beat in eggs, one at a time, until light and fluffy. Sift together flour, baking soda, baking powder, salt, cinnamon, cloves, and nutmeg until well blended.

- Add dry ingredients to butter mixture alternately with pumpkin, blending well after each addition. Begin and end with the flour mixture. Fold in vanilla, nuts (or raisins, if desired), and mix well.

- Pour into loaf pans. Bake at 350 degrees for 60 minutes or until toothpick inserted in center comes out clean.

Yield: 2 (9 x 5-inch) loaves or 6 mini-loaves

Children love this bread, and it's a great way to sneak in some vitamins!

Caraway Irish Soda Bread

Preparation Time: 15 minutes ~ Cook Time: 55 to 60 minutes

2   cups all-purpose unbleached flour
1   cup whole-wheat flour
½   cup sugar
2   teaspoons baking soda
1   teaspoon salt

4   tablespoons cold butter, cut into bits
      (or ¼ cup light vegetable oil; or
      ½ cup applesauce)
1   cup golden raisins
2   teaspoons caraway seeds
1½ cups buttermilk or plain yogurt
      Half-and-half or milk, for brushing

- Butter an 8-inch round pan.

- In a large bowl, whisk together the flours, sugar, baking soda, and salt. Cut in butter with a pastry cutter until the consistency of coarse cornmeal.

- Add raisins and caraway seeds. Toss until coated. Add buttermilk or yogurt. Stir until dough is moistened. Do not overwork dough.

- Knead briefly, sprinkling with additional flour if needed to keep from sticking. Shape dough into a ball and put into prepared pan. Cut a shallow "X" across the top. Brush with half-and-half or milk.

- Bake in the center of the oven at 350 degrees for 55 to 60 minutes, until golden brown. Turn onto a rack and cool completely before slicing.

Yield: 1 large loaf

Best Dill Bread Ever

Preparation Time: 1 and 45 minutes to 2 hours
Cook Time: 40 to 50 minutes

1	cup cottage cheese	1	egg
2	tablespoons sugar	2¼-2½	cups sifted flour
2	tablespoons instant onion	¼	teaspoon baking soda
1-2	tablespoons butter	1	teaspoon salt
1	tablespoon dill weed		Oil, for brushing
1	tablespoon dill seed		Butter
1	package dry yeast		Salt
¼	cup warm water		

- In a large saucepan over low heat, combine cottage cheese, sugar, onion, butter, and dill until butter is melted. Remove from heat and cool to lukewarm.

- While the cheese mixture cools, activate the yeast in warm water. Add the yeast mixture and egg and mix.

- Add the dry ingredients, all at once, beating well. Turn into a greased bowl, cover, and let rise until doubled in size, approximately 45 minutes.

- With lightly oiled hands, punch down dough, shape into a loaf, and place into a well-oiled 1½-quart loaf pan. Let rise 30 to 40 more minutes.

- Brush with oil. Bake at 350 degrees 40 to 50 minutes until a dark, brown crust forms. Remove from oven, rub top with butter, and sprinkle with salt. Leave in pan and cool on a rack.

Yield: 1 loaf

Bread Dough for
Rolls, Pizza Crust, and Focaccia

Preparation Time: 15 to 20 minutes plus refrigeration time
Cook Time: 15 to 25 minutes depending on the use
Prepare ahead.

---

1 teaspoon active dry yeast	1 teaspoon sea salt
1 teaspoon sugar	4 cups (approximately) bread flour
1⅓ cups lukewarm water	(no bleached flour)
2 tablespoons extra virgin olive oil	

- In the bowl of a heavy-duty mixer fitted with a paddle, combine the yeast, sugar, and water, and stir to blend. Let stand until foamy, about 5 minutes. Stir in the oil and salt. Add the flour, a little at a time at the lowest speed until most of the flour has been absorbed and the dough forms a ball.

- Continue to mix at the lowest speed until soft and satiny but still firm, 4 to 5 minutes. Add additional flour, if necessary, to keep the dough from sticking. The dough will be quite soft. Transfer the dough to a bowl. Cover tightly with plastic wrap, and place in refrigerator.

- Let the dough rise in the refrigerator until doubled or tripled in bulk, 8 to 12 hours. The dough can be kept for 2 to 3 days in the refrigerator. Simply punch down the dough as it doubles or triples.

- Proceed with the individual recipes for pizzas, bread, and rolls. Bake at 400 degrees until golden brown between 15 and 25 minutes depending on the use.

Yield: 2 to 3 pizza crusts, 11 x 13-inch jelly-roll-sized focaccia,
or about 2 dozen rolls, depending on size

Country French Bread

Preparation Time: 3 to 4 hours
Cook Time: 12 to 25 minutes

1½ packages dry yeast	1 tablespoon salt
2 cups lukewarm water	Olive oil
1 tablespoon sugar	Yellow cornmeal
5-6 cups bread flour or unbleached plain flour	

- Combine the yeast with the water and sugar in a large bowl, or the mixing bowl of a heavy-duty mixer. Allow to activate until slightly foamy. Meanwhile, in another bowl mix together the flour and salt.

- Add flour to the yeast mixture, 1 cup at a time, until you have a stiff dough.

- If using a mixer, use the dough hook attachment on low speed. Otherwise, knead on a lightly floured surface, adding flour until the dough is no longer sticky and its surface is satiny, about 10 to 15 minutes. Dough has been kneaded enough when a 1-inch ball can be flattened, then stretched with fingers to paper-thinness without tearing.

- Place dough in a bowl lightly coated with olive oil and turn to coat the surface. Cover and let rise in warm place until doubled in bulk, 1½ to 2 hours.

- Punch down dough. Cut in half. Shape into 2 long loaves. Place on a baking sheet that has been lightly sprinkled with cornmeal. Slash the tops of the loaves diagonally 3 or 4 times with a very sharp knife or a single-edged razor blade. Let rise 30 minutes more.

- Brush with water and bake in a preheated 400 degree oven 15 to 25 minutes or until browned and the loaves produce a hollow sound when thumped. For a better crust, throw 6 to 8 ice cubes in the bottom of the oven to produce steam while baking.

Yield: 2 loaves

Homemade Yeast Rolls

Preparation Time: 4 hours ~ Cook Time: 20 minutes
Prepare ahead.

4-5 tablespoons sugar
2 teaspoons salt
4-5 tablespoons shortening
1 cup milk, scalded
1 package yeast

¼ cup lukewarm water
1 egg, beaten
3½ cups flour
½ cup butter or margarine, melted

- Mix sugar, salt, and shortening in milk (temperature of milk to be lukewarm). Mix together yeast and water until thoroughly dissolved. Add warm water mixture to beaten egg.

- Add milk and flour mixture alternately until each is mixed. Set aside and let rise 2 hours. Punch in middle and knead 5 to 10 minutes on floured board.

- Roll out to ¼-inch thickness and spread soft melted butter on top. Cut into circles 2 to 3 inches in diameter with biscuit cutter. Fold full circles in half.

- Set on baking pan, cover, and let rise for another 2 hours. Bake at 400 degrees for 15 to 20 minutes.

Yield: 25 to 30 rolls

Although this takes advance preparation in making, the results are well worth it. The rolls are light and rich to complement any meal!

Pagnotta (Italian Round Bread)

Preparation Time: 1½ hours ~ Cook Time: 55 minutes
Prepare ahead.

---

2   packages yeast
3   cups (approximately) tepid water
8   cups unbleached all-purpose flour
2½ teaspoons coarse salt

2   tablespoons extra virgin olive oil
1   tablespoon safflower or corn oil
      (for baking sheet or stone)

- Dissolve the yeast in ½ cup of the water.

- Electric mixer method: in large mixer bowl, put dissolved yeast, flour, salt, olive oil, and enough of the tepid water to yield a moderately firm dough. Work the dough for about 3 minutes with a dough-hook attachment.

- Hand method: work until the dough becomes elastic, approximately 10 to 15 minutes.

- Form the dough into a round loaf, and place on an oiled baking sheet or stone. Cover with a floured tea towel, and put in a warm place away from drafts, until loaf has doubled in size, approximately 1 hour.

- Preheat oven to 400 degrees. Bake loaf for 55 minutes or until loaf sounds hollow when tapped. Cool on a rack for 3 to 4 hours before using.

Yield: 1 very large loaf

Overnight Rolls

Preparation Time: 15 to 20 minutes plus overnight ~ Cook Time: 30 minutes
Prepare ahead.

1½ sticks butter, divided use
½   cup pecans, chopped
½   cup brown sugar
1   teaspoon cinnamon

½   cup sugar
1   12-count package frozen rolls
      (Rich's, if possible)

- Melt ½ stick butter. Add pecans and brown sugar and pour into bottom of Bundt pan. Melt remaining 1 stick of butter with cinnamon and ½ cup sugar. Coat frozen rolls in mixture. Place pan in cold oven before bed. Cover with a towel.

- In the morning, remove towel and turn on oven. Bake at 350 degrees for 30 minutes.

Serves: 8

Barbecue Beef Brisket Sandwiches

Preparation Time: 20 minutes ~ Bake or cook Time: 3½ hours
Prepare ahead.

1	2-pound brisket of beef	½	teaspoon garlic powder
½	teaspoon liquid smoke	8-10	poppy seed sandwich rolls
1	teaspoon salt	2	cups barbecue sauce
½	teaspoon paprika		(homemade, or use K.C. Masterpiece
½	teaspoon dry mustard		cut with vinegar and spiced up)

- Place brisket in roasting pan and brush with liquid smoke. Combine the salt and spices in a small bowl and mix well. Rub into brisket.

- Cover roasting pan and bake at 325 degrees until fork tender, about 3½ hours. Remove the pan from the oven, and use 2 forks to pull meat apart in pan juices. Shred coarsely.

- Put 2 tablespoons of barbecue sauce on each roll followed by beef and more sauce as desired. Serve with additional sauce on the side. Great served on poppy seed rolls. Men love this one!

Serves: 8

Barbecue Sauce

2	tablespoons vegetable oil	1	cup ketchup
½	cup onion, chopped	½	cup malt vinegar
2	tablespoons garlic, minced	¼	cup soy sauce
1	teaspoon ground cumin	½	cup dark brown sugar
¼	teaspoon cayenne pepper	2	tablespoons Worcestershire sauce

- Combine over medium heat and simmer.

Yield: about 2 cups

Cuban Sandwiches

Preparation Time: 20 minutes ~ Cook Time: 5 to 10 minutes

1½ loaves Cuban bread (Italian will do)
Mustard and butter
¼ pound Italian salami
¾ pound baked ham

½ pound roast pork
¼ pound sliced Swiss cheese
(Muenster is nice, too)
Dill pickles, sliced lengthwise

- Cut the bread in 6 pieces, approximately 8 inches long. Split lengthwise and spread mustard on one piece, and butter on the other.

- Divide the salami, ham, pork, cheese, and pickles among the 6 sandwiches, arranging in layers on the bread. Wrap each sandwich in a paper napkin and secure with a toothpick.

- Flavor is improved by warming in the oven before serving.

Serves: 6

Hartsville Sandwich Filling

Preparation Time: 15 to 20 minutes

---

1 4.75-ounce bottle pimento-stuffed olives
2 hard-boiled eggs

1 cup pecans
2-4 tablespoons mayonnaise

- In a blender or food processor, mix first 3 ingredients to a puree. Add enough mayonnaise for a smooth spreading consistency.

- Use ¼-inch thickness when spreading for sandwiches.

Yield: Filling for 6 to 8 sandwiches

Italian Grilled Veggie Hoagies

Preparation Time: 30 minutes ~ Cook Time: 20 minutes

4	Italian hoagie rolls
4	portobello mushrooms
2	red bell peppers
1	red onion
	Olive oil

	Dijon mustard
4	slices provolone or mozzarella cheese
	Fresh basil leaves
	Salt, pepper, garlic powder, to taste

- Slice the rolls lengthwise.

- Slice vegetables and brush with oil (except peppers - no oil) and grill or roast under broiler until done. Or sauté in 1 tablespoon olive oil, approximately 10 minutes over medium heat.

- To roast peppers, cook until skin is blackened on all sides, and then cool in covered container. Remove skin, slice into halves, and remove seeds and veins.

- Coat one side of roll with mustard, and one side with olive oil. Layer mushroom, peppers, onions, cheese, and basil. Season with salt, pepper, and garlic powder.

- Warm in a 350 degree oven until cheese is melted, about 5 minutes.

Serves: 4

Open-Faced Ham Sandwiches

Preparation Time: 30 minutes ~ Cook Time: 3 to 5 minutes

8 ounces cream cheese, softened
½ cup butter or margarine, softened
½ cup Parmesan cheese, grated
1 teaspoon paprika
½ teaspoon dried whole oregano
Dash garlic powder

4 English muffins, split
8 slices cooked ham (round, thinly sliced deli works well, but use several slices since it's thin)
8 slices tomatoes
Fresh parsley sprigs

- Combine cream cheese and butter; blend until smooth; stir in cheese, paprika, oregano, and garlic powder.

- Spread 1 tablespoon of mixture on center of each muffin. Top each with ham and tomato slice. Spoon remaining mixture on top.

- Broil in oven until golden brown. Garnish with parsley sprig. Delicious!

Yield: 8 sandwiches

Party Ham Sandwiches

Preparation Time: 15 minutes ~ Cook Time: 15 minutes

⅓ pound butter, softened
3 tablespoons poppy seeds
3 tablespoons prepared mustard
1 teaspoon Worcestershire sauce

1 small onion, finely diced
3 pans party rolls (20 rolls per pan)
1 pound baked ham, thinly sliced
⅓ pound Swiss or Havarti cheese, thinly sliced

- Blend first 5 ingredients together. Cut each whole bun and spread with mixture. Layer ham and cheese on the buns. Put top on. Then separate the individual rolls.

- Wrap in foil. Bake at 400 degrees for 15 minutes. These can be made ahead and frozen.

Yield: 60 sandwiches

Chilled Cherry Soup

Preparation Time: 5 minutes
May prepare ahead.

2	pounds canned sour cherries, drained	1	tablespoon flour
1	cup sugar	1	cup heavy cream
1	stick cinnamon	1	cup red wine
3	cups water		

- Mix all ingredients together. Heat until thickened, stirring constantly, then chill. Does not freeze well.

Serves: 6

Cucumber Dill Soup

Preparation Time: 15 minutes
Cook Time: 45 minutes plus 1 hour refrigeration time
May prepare ahead.

3	large cucumbers, peeled, seeded, and chopped	3	tablespoons butter
1	large white onion, chopped	3	tablespoons flour
3	cups chicken stock, divided use	1	cup sour cream or plain yogurt
	Fresh or dried dill weed	1	cup whipping cream (do not substitute)
	White pepper		Fresh dill sprigs
			Lemon slices, cut very thin

- Place cucumbers, onion, and 1½ cups of stock in a heavy covered saucepan. Heat on high until boiling. Reduce heat and simmer, covered for 30 minutes.

- Puree in blender or processor. Add generous pinch of dill weed and white pepper to taste.

- Melt butter over low heat and whisk in flour slowly. Slowly whisk in remaining stock and cook until slightly thickened. Remove from heat and add cucumber puree. Blend in sour cream or yogurt.

- Whip the cream with chilled beaters until soft peaks form. Fold into soup gently. Chill at least 1 hour, and garnish with dill sprigs and lemon slices. Do not freeze.

Serves: 6

Fruit and Champagne Soup

Preparation Time: 25 minutes
Prepare ahead.

2	ripe peaches, pared and sliced	3	tablespoons sugar
1	16-ounce can Bing cherries, reserve liquid	2	tablespoons cornstarch
1	16-ounce can tart or pie cherries, reserve liquid	⅓	cup Cointreau or similar orange liqueur
1	teaspoon orange peel	2	navel oranges, peeled and sectioned
1	teaspoon cinnamon	1	750-ml bottle dry champagne

- Combine peaches, cherries, and their juice in a large saucepan and add spices, sugar, and cornstarch.

- Heat over low heat until mixture boils and thickens. Remove from heat and pour into large bowl. Add Cointreau and oranges.

- Refrigerate until well chilled. Add 3 ounces of champagne to each portion just before serving.

Serves: 8

Creamy Crab Stew

Preparation Time: 15 minutes   ~   Cook Time: 30 minutes

½	cup butter	½	bay leaf
¾	cup carrots, finely chopped	1	tablespoon fresh ground black pepper
¾	cup celery, finely chopped	1	teaspoon salt
1	cup onion, finely chopped	⅛	teaspoon cayenne pepper
¼	cup flour	1	teaspoon Old Bay seasoning
4	cups milk	1	tablespoon Worcestershire sauce
4	cups heavy cream or half-and-half	1	pound crabmeat

- Melt butter in a large saucepan. Cook carrots, celery, and onion over moderately low heat, stirring until softened, about 5 minutes. Add flour and cook, stirring, for 3 minutes.

- Add milk, cream, bay leaf, pepper, salt, cayenne, Old Bay, and Worcestershire sauce. Bring to a boil; reduce heat and simmer, stirring until slightly thickened, about 8 to 10 minutes.

- Add crabmeat and cook, while stirring for 3 minutes. Remove bay leaf before serving.

Serves: 6 to 8

Gazpacho

Preparation Time: 15 minutes ~ Chill Time: 2 hours
Prepare ahead.

1	48-ounce can tomato juice, divided use	2	teaspoons Greek seasoning
1	medium red onion, chopped	1	tablespoon lemon or lime juice
1	red bell pepper, seeded and chopped	1	tablespoon olive oil
1	green bell pepper, seeded and chopped	3	ripe tomatoes, peeled and seeded
3	cloves garlic	2	cucumbers, peeled and seeded
2	tablespoons red wine vinegar		Dash cayenne pepper, optional
1	tablespoon cilantro, chopped	1	cup sour cream

- Put half of juice in blender along with other ingredients except sour cream. Blend until smooth. Pour into container for refrigeration.

- Add remaining juice and blend. Chill 2 hours. Do not freeze.

- Serve with a dollop of sour cream on top.

Serves: 6

Oyster Soup

Preparation Time: 15 minutes

1	quart oysters with juice	Pepper, to taste
1	gallon whole milk	Oyster crackers
½	stick butter	

- Heat oysters with juice until edges curl.

- Heat milk and butter in a separate pan. Combine with oysters when ready to serve.

- Add pepper to taste. Top with crackers.

Serves: 12 to 16

Shrimp Bisque

Preparation Time: 20 minutes
Cook Time: 20 to 25 minutes

1	pound fresh or frozen shrimp, shelled
1	cup onion, diced
¾	cup apple, peeled and shredded
2	tablespoons butter or oil
1	tablespoon flour
1½	cups water
1	teaspoon fresh lemon juice
1	piece lemon peel (2 inches)
⅛	teaspoon curry powder
⅓	teaspoon dried dill
¼	teaspoon salt
¼	teaspoon pepper
2	tablespoons dry white wine
1	cup half-and-half
	Lemon slices, thin

- Rinse shrimp. Sauté onions and apples in butter or oil for 10 minutes. Sprinkle in flour and stir 1 minute. Add water, lemon juice, lemon peel, curry, dill, salt, pepper, and wine. Simmer, covered, for 5 minutes while mixture thickens.

- Add shrimp and half-and-half and simmer gently until shrimp turn pink. (Do not over-cook.) Remove lemon peel.

- Puree ⅓ of the soup in a food processor or blender and return to the pot. Serve immediately with lemon slices.

Serves: 4 to 6

Shrimp and Corn Soup

Preparation Time: 45 minutes (more if you need to peel the shrimp).
Cook Time: 30 minutes

¼ cup vegetable oil	1 20-ounce can tomato puree
3 tablespoons flour	1 15-ounce can cream-style corn
1 medium onion, finely chopped	1-1½ cups hot water
1 pound raw shrimp, peeled (do not use cooked shrimp)	Salt, black pepper, and red pepper to taste
1 teaspoon garlic, minced	

- In a frying pan over low heat, pour oil and stir in flour to make a roux. When slightly brown, add onion and shrimp and fry very slightly. Add garlic and stir. Remove from heat.

- In a large saucepan, heat tomato puree and cream style corn. Add shrimp mixture and reduce heat. Cook very slowly for 10 to 15 minutes.

- Add hot water and stir well. Continue to cook very slowly until soup is heated through. Serve immediately.

Serves: 6

Carrot Soup

Preparation Time: 30 minutes ~ Cook Time: 45 minutes
May prepare ahead.

1 large onion, chopped	6 large carrots, peeled and sliced
3 cloves garlic, minced	1 large potato, peeled and sliced
6 tablespoons butter, divided use	1 bay leaf
½ teaspoon ground thyme	1 teaspoon salt
3 cans chicken broth	Dash white pepper
3 cans water	

- Sauté onion and garlic in 2 tablespoons butter. Add thyme. Add chicken broth, water, carrots, potato, bay leaf, salt, and pepper. Simmer 45 minutes. Cool.

- Discard bay leaf and puree in blender.

- Before serving, reheat, adding remaining 4 tablespoons butter.

Serves: 6 to 8

Seafood Cornucopia Stew

Cook Time: 3½ to 4 hours

¼   cup vegetable oil
¼   cup all-purpose flour
2   stalks celery, chopped
1   medium onion, chopped
½   green pepper, chopped
½   red pepper, chopped
1   clove garlic, minced
1   pound fresh okra, sliced
      (or thawed, frozen okra)
1   tablespoon vegetable oil
2   cups chicken broth
1½ cups water
1   cup shrimp stock (see below)
¼   cup Worcestershire sauce
¼   cup ketchup
1   teaspoon hot sauce, or to taste

Dash Old Bay seasoning
1   8-ounce can chopped tomatoes, not
      drained
1   teaspoon salt
1   teaspoon pepper
1   slice bacon, chopped
1   bay leaf
¼   teaspoon dried rosemary
¼   teaspoon red pepper flakes, or to taste
1   pound medium shrimp, peeled, de-veined
      and cut into medium-sized pieces
      (reserve shells for shrimp stock)
1   pound fresh "special" crabmeat, picked
      through (claw meat may be substituted)
6-8 ounces shucked oysters, not drained
      (optional)
      Cooked white rice

- Combine oil and flour in a large soup pot, stirring occasionally over medium heat until roux is dark caramel colored, about 15 to 20 minutes. Stir in celery, onion, green and red pepper, and garlic, and cook over low to medium heat for 45 to 50 minutes, stirring occasionally.

- In a separate pan, fry okra at medium heat with 1 tablespoon of vegetable oil until browned, 12 to 15 minutes.

- Add okra to stew, stirring occasionally for 3 to 5 minutes. Add broth, water, and shrimp stock and the next 11 ingredients. Simmer, uncovered, for 2½ hours, stirring occasionally.

- Add shrimp, crab, and oysters, if desired, and stir for 10 minutes. Remove bay leaf. Serve warm over cooked rice in bowls.

Serves: 6 to 8

Shrimp Stock: Put shrimp shells, 2 cups water, and 1 large stalk chopped celery in a medium-sized pot. Bring to a boil, cover, and simmer for 3 to 5 minutes. Let stand 10 to 15 minutes and strain stock into a bowl.

Light Corn Chowder

Preparation Time: 5 to 10 minutes ~ Cook Time: 45 minutes

Vegetable cooking spray
1 cup onion, chopped
6 cups corn kernels, frozen
(a mixture of yellow and white is best),
divided use
3 cups canned chicken broth
½ cup red bell pepper, chopped

½ teaspoon dried oregano
½ teaspoon dried thyme
⅛ teaspoon white pepper
Cayenne pepper, to taste
1 tablespoon fresh basil or flat leaf parsley,
chopped
4 teaspoons bacon, cooked and crumbled,
optional

- Spray and preheat soup pot (medium heat) with the vegetable spray. Sauté the onion until translucent, about 5 minutes. Add 4 cups of the corn and sauté until it softens for about 10 minutes. Add 2 cups of the chicken broth and cook the corn for 20 minutes.

- Transfer to a blender or a food processor and puree until smooth. Return the puree to the pot on medium-low heat. Add the remaining ingredients and cook for another 10 minutes. Divide into 4 portions and garnish with basil (and bacon, if desired).

Serves: 4

Sausage and Corn Chowder

Preparation Time: 30 minutes ~ Cook Time: 30 minutes

1 pound mild sausage
1 small onion, chopped
4 cups potatoes, cubed
1 teaspoon salt
1 tablespoon parsley
1 teaspoon basil

⅛ teaspoon pepper
2 cups water
1 16-ounce can creamed corn
1 16-ounce can whole kernel corn
1 12-ounce can evaporated milk

- Brown sausage and onion. Drain excess fat. Set aside. Cook potatoes, salt, parsley, basil, pepper, and water and cook on stove top for 15 minutes.

- Add canned corn and milk. Add meat and onion. Heat together 5 to 10 minutes and serve.

Serves: 6

French Onion Soup

Preparation Time: 10 minutes ~ Cook Time: 1 hour and 30 minutes

---

3 tablespoons butter, plus additional for spreading on bread
1 tablespoon olive oil, plus additional for spreading on bread
1½ pounds onions, very thinly sliced
1 teaspoon salt
½ teaspoon sugar
3 tablespoons flour
2 quarts hot beef broth
1 cup dry red wine
1 bay leaf
½ teaspoon sage
1 loaf sturdy French bread or 1 package toasted baguette slices
1½ cups Swiss and Parmesan cheeses, grated and mixed
   Salt and pepper, to taste
¼ cup cognac

- Melt butter and oil in a soup pot. Add onions and stir to coat. Cover and cook over medium-low heat for 15 to 20 minutes, stirring occasionally.

- Uncover pot, raise heat to medium-high, and stir in the salt and sugar. Cook for about 30 minutes more, stirring very often, until onions are a golden brown. Be careful not to burn.

- Lower heat to medium and add flour to make into a paste with the onions. (Add a bit more butter, if necessary.) Cook slowly, stirring continuously, for 2 minutes. Remove from heat.

- Pour in a cup of the hot broth, stirring with a whisk to blend. Add the rest of the broth, wine, bay leaf, and sage. Bring to a simmer and cook for another 30 to 40 minutes.

- Meanwhile, slice the bread into 1 inch slices. Brush lightly with oil or butter. On a cookie sheet, bake in a single layer for 15 to 20 minutes at 325 degrees, or until they begin to brown. Then cook 15 to 20 minutes on the other side. Top the croûtes with the cheese and broil for just long enough to melt the cheese completely (watch carefully).

- Season the soup to taste, and add the cognac. May be frozen before adding the cognac. Serve in bowls and top with the croûtes.

Serves: 6

Baked Potato Soup

Preparation Time: 1 hour ~ Cook Time: 1 to 2 hours

4	large baking potatoes
⅔	cup butter or margarine
⅔	cup all-purpose flour
6	cups milk
	Salt and pepper, to taste
4	green onions, chopped, divided use

12 slices bacon, cooked and crumbled, divided use

1¼ cups Cheddar cheese, shredded (5 ounces), divided use

1 8-ounce container sour cream

- Wash potatoes and prick several times with a fork. Bake at 400 degrees for 1 hour or until done. Let cool. Cut potatoes in half lengthwise and scoop out the pulp. Mash and set aside (discard skins).

- Melt butter in a heavy saucepan over low heat. Add flour, stirring constantly. Gradually add milk; cook over medium heat, stirring constantly until mixture is thickened and bubbly. Add potato pulp, salt, pepper, 2 tablespoons green onions, ½ cup bacon, and 1 cup cheese. Cook until thoroughly heated.

- Stir in sour cream and add extra milk, if necessary, for desired thickness. Serve with remaining onion, bacon, and cheese.

Serves: 6

Cream of Spinach Soup

Preparation Time: 20 to 25 minutes ~ Cook Time: 25 to 30 minutes

1   tablespoon oil
2   medium-sized onions, chopped
3   cloves garlic (or less), minced
1½ pounds fresh spinach (18 ounces cleaned)
       or 1 frozen package
2¾ cups chicken broth

3   tablespoons white wine
¾   teaspoon lemon zest, grated
½   teaspoon salt
⅛   teaspoon nutmeg
⅛   teaspoon black pepper
1½ cups half-and-half

- Sauté onion and garlic in oil for 10 minutes. Add spinach and cook for 5 minutes.

- Add chicken broth, wine, lemon zest, salt, nutmeg, and pepper and simmer for 3 minutes.

- Put in a food processor or blender and puree. Return to pot and stir in half-and-half.

Serves: 8

This soup can be refrigerated up to 2 days. It is actually best if prepared a day ahead, which helps with planning.

Tomato Bisque

Preparation Time: 30 minutes   ~   Cooking Time: 1 hour and 15 minutes

½	cup butter	1	teaspoon marjoram
½	cup celery, chopped	1	teaspoon basil
½	cup carrots, chopped	3	bay leaves
1	cup onion, chopped	¼	teaspoon paprika
½	cup flour	¼	teaspoon pepper
4	cups chicken broth	½	teaspoon curry powder
3	16-ounce cans chopped tomatoes, with juice	3	teaspoons tomato paste
2	teaspoons sugar	2	cups heavy cream (or 1 cup heavy cream and 1 cup of skim milk)

- Sauté celery, carrots, and onions in butter until soft. Stir in flour and cook 1 minute.

- Slowly add chicken broth and stir well. Add tomatoes, sugar, marjoram, basil, bay leaves, paprika, pepper, curry powder, and tomato paste.

- Cover and cook over low heat for about 1 hour, or until carrots are very soft.

- Remove from heat and puree in blender. Return to stove, stir in cream, and heat through.

Serves: 6

Chili with Something Extra

Preparation Time: 20 minutes ~ Cook Time: 1 hour and 45 minutes

3	pounds ground chuck		2	14.5-ounce cans stewed tomatoes
1	pound Italian sausage, hot or mild		1	29-ounce can tomato sauce
1	onion, chopped		1	12-ounce can beer
½	cup green pepper, chopped		1	6-ounce can tomato paste
½	cup celery, chopped		1½-2	tablespoons chili powder, or to taste
1	clove garlic, minced		1	hot pepper, seeded and diced
4	15.5-ounce cans kidney beans, not drained		¼	teaspoon oregano

- In separate pans, cook ground chuck and Italian sausage. Drain thoroughly.

- Combine all other ingredients in a large soup pot. Add meats to this mixture and stir well.

- Cook approximately 1½ hours.

Serves: 10

Serving suggestions: Top with shredded cheese and chopped onions. Wonderful served over rice or with tortilla chips.

Cincinnati Chili

Preparation Time: 15 minutes ~ Cook Time: 1 hour and 15 minutes

1	pound ground round beef	1	teaspoon cider vinegar
1½	cups onion, chopped	¾	teaspoon ground cinnamon
2	garlic cloves, minced	½	teaspoon salt
1¾	cups low-salt chicken broth	¼	teaspoon ground allspice
½	cup water	1	bay leaf
2	tablespoons chili powder	1	15-ounce can kidney beans, optional
1	teaspoon oregano	1	15-ounce can chopped or diced tomatoes with juice
1	teaspoon ground cumin		
1	teaspoon Worcestershire sauce	5	cups hot cooked spaghetti

- Combine ground round, onion, and garlic in a medium saucepan. Cook over medium heat until meat is browned. Drain well.

- Add chicken broth and all ingredients except spaghetti. Bring to a boil. Reduce heat and simmer 1 hour, stirring occasionally. Discard bay leaf. Spoon spaghetti onto plates and top with chili.

Serves: 6

Variations:

For 3-way chili, add shredded sharp Cheddar cheese and oyster crackers for garnish.

For 4-way chili, add chopped onion for garnish.

For 5-way chili, add 1 can (15 ounces) kidney beans.

Fusion Chicken and White Bean Soup

Preparation Time: 20 minutes ~ Cook Time: 1 hour and 15 minutes

---

¼   cup olive oil
2   whole boneless, skinless chicken breasts, cubed
1   large onion, chopped
6-8 small carrots, coarsely chopped
2-3 cloves garlic, minced
1   4-ounce can chopped green chilies
½   teaspoon white pepper

½   teaspoon cayenne pepper
      Salt, to taste
½   teaspoon parsley, chopped
1   teaspoon cumin
2   14.5-ounce cans chicken stock or broth
2   19-ounce cans cannellini beans
      Sour cream and grated Cheddar cheese
         for garnish

- Sauté chicken, onion, carrots, and garlic in oil until tender. Add chilies and seasonings.

- Add chicken broth and simmer approximately 30 to 40 minutes, adding water as needed to maintain soupy consistency.

- Add beans and simmer for 20 to 30 minutes more. Serve with a dollop of sour cream and grated Cheddar cheese.

Serves: 6 to 8

Taco Soup

Preparation Time: 5 minutes ~ Cook Time: 1 hour and 10 minutes

1   pound ground beef or turkey
1   1-pound can pinto or red beans
1   1-pound can whole corn
1   1-pound can black beans
1   1-pound can stewed tomatoes

1   10-ounce can Rotel tomatoes
1   12-ounce can beer
1   package taco seasoning
1   package ranch dressing mix

- Brown beef or turkey and drain. Add all ingredients into a large pot and simmer for 1 hour. Serve with corn chips or corn bread.

Serves: 8

Variation: For a very busy day, add all ingredients to a crock pot and cook on low for 6 to 8 hours.

Mulligatawny Soup

Preparation Time: 15 minutes ~ Cook Time: 70 minutes

3   pounds chicken, cut up
¼   cup butter
¼   cup bell pepper, chopped
¼   cup carrots, chopped
2   Granny Smith apples, peeled, cored, and chopped
1   tablespoon flour

1   tablespoon curry powder (or more to taste)
2-3 quarts chicken broth
2   cloves
    Pinch mace
2   teaspoons salt
    Pinch pepper
1½ cups Basmati rice

- Brown chicken on all sides in butter. Add bell pepper, carrots, and apple. Cook on medium-high for 5 minutes.

- Combine flour and curry powder. Sprinkle over chicken and vegetables. Mix well. Add chicken broth, cloves, mace, salt, and pepper.

- Cook until chicken is done. Remove chicken and add rice. Dice chicken and return to pot. Serve when rice is cooked, approximately 20 minutes.

Serves: 6 to 8

Can be made with precooked chicken or leftover turkey.

White Bean Chicken Chili

Preparation Time: 45 minutes (plus soak beans overnight)
Cook Time: 2 hours

Beans

1	pound white navy beans	7	cups chicken stock
1	small red bell pepper, diced	2	cloves garlic, minced
1	small green pepper, diced	1	tablespoon cumin
1	medium onion, chopped	1	tablespoon chili powder
2	tablespoons olive oil	3	Roma tomatoes, chopped

Chicken

3	whole chicken breasts, boned and skinned	1	teaspoon cumin
2	tablespoons olive oil	1	clove garlic, minced
1	teaspoon chili powder	2	tablespoons cilantro, chopped

Garnish

	Salsa for topping	Fresh cilantro, chopped
4	quesadillas	

- For the beans, soak overnight in water to cover. Drain. Over low heat, stir peppers and onion in olive oil for 2 minutes. Add beans and sauté over medium heat for 5 minutes, stirring constantly. Add the chicken stock, garlic, cumin, and chili powder. Simmer, uncovered, until the beans are tender, about 2 hours, adding more broth if necessary. Stir in the tomatoes and cook for 15 more minutes.

- For the chicken, rub chicken breasts with oil and season with remaining spices. Roast at 350 degrees for 30 minutes. Cool slightly and slice thin.

- To serve, place generous portion of beans in soup bowl. Place chicken on the top. Garnish with salsa and warm quesadilla. Garnish with cilantro.

Serves: 6 to 8

Make quesadillas by topping a soft flour tortilla with ¼ cup grated Cheddar cheese, 2 tablespoons sour cream and folding into quarters.

Cheese Soup

Preparation Time: 10 minutes ~ Cook Time: 20 to 25 minutes

¼ cup butter
1 cup onions, finely diced
1 cup celery, finely diced
¼ cup flour
1½ tablespoons cornstarch
4 cups milk, room temperature
4 cups chicken stock, room temperature

⅛ teaspoon baking soda
1 pound Old English or Kraft American cheese, cubed
White pepper and salt, to taste
Dash cayenne pepper
1 tablespoon dried parsley
Paprika

- Melt butter and sauté vegetables until tender. Stir in flour and cornstarch and cook until bubbly. Add stock and milk gradually stirring with a whisk, blending into a smooth sauce.

- Add baking soda and cheese cubes. Stir until thickened. Season with salt, pepper, and cayenne. Add parsley. Garnish with paprika.

Serves: 6 to 8

If you need to reheat, do so in a double boiler. Don't boil.

Veal Meatball Soup

Preparation Time: 30 minutes ~ Cook Time: 40 minutes

1 pound ground veal (or turkey)
½ teaspoon salt
¼ teaspoon pepper
2 egg whites at room temperature, beaten lightly
Dash nutmeg

2 teaspoons fresh lemon zest, grated
2 teaspoons fresh parsley, chopped
8 cups chicken broth
¾ cup white rice, uncooked
Juice of 1 lemon
6 cups fresh spinach, coarsely chopped

- Mix veal, salt, pepper, egg whites, nutmeg, lemon zest, and parsley. Form into small balls, about 1 to 1½ inches in diameter. Bring broth to a boil. Add rice and cook 10 minutes.

- Add meatballs and lemon juice and boil gently 10 to 15 minutes. Add spinach and simmer 10 more minutes.

Serves: 4

Spinach, Sausage, and Pasta Soup

Preparation Time: 30 minutes ~ Cook Time: 45 minutes

1	pound sweet Italian sausage links (remove casings)	½	teaspoon salt
1	tablespoon olive oil	3	15-ounce cans great Northern or cannellini beans, drained and rinsed
2	medium-sized onions, chopped	1	rounded cup ditalini or tubetti pasta
2	garlic cloves, crushed	½	10-ounce bag spinach, stems removed, leaves cut into 1-inch strips
1	28-ounce can plum tomatoes in juice		Parmesan cheese for garnish
1	14-ounce can chicken broth		

- Heat 5-quart Dutch oven over medium heat and add sausage. Cook until brown, breaking up meat with a spoon. Remove meat to a bowl and drain on a paper towel.

- Add olive oil to drippings and cook onions until tender. Add garlic and cook 1 minute.

- Add tomatoes with juice, chicken broth, and salt and simmer for 15 minutes.

- Add rinsed beans. Heat to boiling and simmer 15 more minutes. Add sausage and heat through.

- Meanwhile, cook pasta according to directions. Drain and set aside. Just before serving, stir in spinach and cooked pasta. Serve with Parmesan cheese (optional).

Serves: 8

Entrées

Elementary to
Exemplary

Entrées

Blackened Chicken
with Tomato-Olive Coulis

Preparation Time: 40 minutes ~ Cook Time: 30 minutes

Chicken

¾   **teaspoon oregano**
¾   **teaspoon garlic powder**
½   **teaspoon cayenne pepper**
½   **teaspoon black pepper**

3   **whole chicken breasts, halved, boned, and skinned**
2   **tablespoons olive oil**

Tomato-Olive Coulis

3   **tablespoons butter**
½   **cup onion, chopped**
1½   **teaspoons garlic, chopped**
1¼   **cups tomatoes, peeled, seeded, and chopped**

½   **cup chicken broth**
12   **black olives, pitted and sliced**
6   **green olives, pitted and sliced**

- About 40 minutes before cooking, in a small bowl, mix oregano, garlic powder, cayenne, and black pepper. Rub mixture on both sides of the chicken breasts. Cover, let stand 30 minutes.

- For tomato-olive coulis, melt butter in large skillet over medium-high heat. Add onion, sauté until softened about 5 minutes. Add garlic and tomatoes and sauté 2 minutes. Add stock and olives; cook 5 minutes, stirring frequently. Set aside; keep warm.

- Heat olive oil in large heavy skillet over high heat. Add chicken; sauté until golden brown, about 5 to 10 minutes per side or until no longer pink in the center.

- Remove chicken to warm platter; tent with foil to keep warm. Pour any juices from chicken platter into coulis sauce mix. Spoon coulis over chicken to serve.

Serves: 6

Broiled Chicken with Herb Butter

Preparation Time: 15 minutes ~ Cook Time: 45 minutes

3	tablespoons butter, softened	¼	teaspoon salt
3	tablespoons shallots or onion, minced	¼	teaspoon pepper
½	teaspoon thyme	1½	teaspoons lemon peel, grated
½	teaspoon rubbed sage	3-3½	pound frying chicken, quartered
1	teaspoon dried tarragon	¼	cup dry white wine or ¼ cup chicken broth

- In a small pan, combine butter, shallots, thyme, sage, tarragon, salt, pepper, and lemon peel. Set aside.

- Rinse chicken and pat dry. With a sharp knife, cut small slits in skin over breasts, thighs, and meaty part of wing. Push small amounts of butter mixture through slits between skin and flesh, using about ¾ of the butter mixture.

- Melt remaining butter mixture and add the wine. Brush with butter/wine mixture. Remove from heat. Arrange chicken quarters, skin side down, on a rack in a broiler pan. Broil 6 to 8 inches below heat for 15 minutes. Turn chicken over and continue to broil, brushing occasionally until meat is no longer pink. Total cooking time is 30 to 45 minutes.

Serves: 4

Chicken and
Wild Rice Casserole

Preparation Time: 20 minutes ~ Cook Time: 30 to 40 minutes
May prepare ahead.

2	cups cooked long grain and wild rice	1	10½-ounce can cream of mushroom soup
4	large chicken breasts, cooked and cut into bite-sized pieces	1	4-ounce can sliced mushrooms
		1	8-ounce container sour cream

- Mix all of the ingredients together and put into a casserole dish (2½ to 3-quart size).

- Bake at 350 degrees for 30 to 40 minutes.

Serves: 6 to 8

Chicken Bundles

Preparation Time: 30 to 45 minutes ~ Cook Time: 25 minutes

3 tablespoons butter or margarine	⅛ teaspoon pepper
3 tablespoons flour	⅛ teaspoon thyme
1½ cups milk, warmed	⅛ teaspoon basil
1½ cups Cheddar cheese, shredded	½ teaspoon lemon juice
2 cups 40% bran flakes, divided use	1 pound boneless chicken, cooked and cubed
5 tablespoons butter or margarine, melted, divided use	2 cans crescent dinner rolls

- Combine margarine and flour in saucepan. Cook 2 minutes. Add milk and cook until thickened. Stir in cheese until melted.

- Combine 1 cup of the cereal, 3 tablespoons butter, and next 5 ingredients. Crush remaining 1 cup cereal to crumbs and set aside.

- Separate rolls into 8 rectangles (2 triangles each), pressing together perforations. Place chicken mixture in center of each. Gather corners together forming a ball, pinch to seal.

- Roll bundles in remaining 2 tablespoons butter and then in crushed crumbs. Slightly flatten and place on ungreased baking sheet. Bake at 350 degrees for 25 minutes. Serve with cheese sauce.

Serves: 8

Roast meat or fowl will carve more easily and the juices will be more evenly distributed if allowed to stand at room temperature for about 15 minutes.

Chicken Cordon Bleu

Preparation Time: 15 minutes
Cook Time: 15 to 20 minutes

4 skinless, boned chicken breasts	1 teaspoon warm water
Salt and pepper, to taste	⅓ cup bread crumbs
4 slices ham	3 tablespoons parsley, chopped
4 slices provolone cheese	1 teaspoon Italian seasoning
1 tablespoon mayonnaise	

- Flatten chicken between sheets of waxed paper to about ¼-inch thickness. Season with salt and pepper. Place slice of ham and cheese on each breast. Roll up and secure with toothpicks.

- Combine mayonnaise and water; brush on all sides of chicken roll. Mix bread crumbs, parsley, and Italian seasoning together. Roll chicken in breadcrumb mixture to coat.

- Place on lightly greased baking sheet. Bake at 450 degrees for 15 to 20 minutes, or until chicken is done.

Serves: 4

This is a fun recipe because you can vary the cheese or the ham you use for a different flavor. It is always a winner!

Chicken Fajitas with Peppers

Preparation Time: 1 hour
Cook Time: 20 to 30 minutes

¼ cup cooking oil
¼ cup vinegar
4 cloves garlic, minced
1 fresh jalapeño pepper, seeded and chopped
2 tablespoons fresh oregano or 2 teaspoons dried crushed oregano
2 teaspoons seasoned salt
1 teaspoon ground cumin

2 large chicken breasts, cut into thin 3-inch strips
1 red sweet pepper, cut into strips
1 green sweet pepper, cut into strips
1 yellow sweet pepper, cut into strips
1 red onion, cut into thin wedges
16 8-inch flour tortillas
1-2 tablespoons olive oil
Salsa
Guacamole

- For marinade, in a large mixing bowl combine cooking oil, vinegar, garlic, jalapeño peppers, oregano, seasoned salt, and cumin.

- Pour half of the marinade into another bowl. Add chicken strips to one bowl of marinade. Add pepper and onion to the other bowl. Cover and marinate both bowls at room temperature for up to 30 minutes or in the refrigerator for 2 to 24 hours.

- Wrap tortillas in a stack in foil. Heat in oven at 350 degrees for 10 minutes to soften.

- Meanwhile, drain vegetables and chicken. On medium-high heat, cook and stir vegetables in oil about 3 minutes. Remove from skillet, add more oil to skillet and stir-fry chicken.

- Serve chicken and vegetables in warmed tortillas with salsa and guacamole, if desired.

Serves: 8

Chicken Paprika

Preparation Time: 10 minutes
Cook Time: 1 hour and 30 minutes

3	pounds chicken, dark meat		2	cups onions, finely chopped
	Salt and pepper, to taste		3	tablespoons sweet paprika
2	tablespoons butter or cooking spray		1	cup sour cream

- Sprinkle the chicken on all sides with salt and pepper. Set aside.

- In a Dutch oven, on medium heat, melt the butter and add the onions. Cook stirring often, until wilted. Cook without browning, until most of the liquid from the onions evaporates.

- Add the chicken and stir briefly. Cover and cook gently over very low heat until the chicken gives up some of its liquid, about 10 minutes.

- Sprinkle the chicken with paprika. Cover and cook for about 1 hour until chicken is tender.

- Remove from heat. With a slotted spoon, put chicken in a casserole dish. Add the sour cream to the remaining liquid, stirring with a whisk. Pour over chicken. Serve over basmati rice.

Serves: 4 to 6

To reduce fat content, use cooking spray instead of butter, skinned chicken, and no-fat sour cream. When preparing ahead or freezing, do not add sour cream until just before serving.

Grilled Cumin Chicken

Preparation Time: 15 minutes plus 2 to 3 hours refrigeration time
Cook Time: 60 to 80 minutes

1	chicken, cut up, with skin on	1	tablespoon black pepper
	Juice of 3 lemons	2½	teaspoons celery salt
2	tablespoons oil	¼	teaspoon cayenne pepper
2	tablespoons ground cumin		(or more, to taste)

- Place chicken in a large shallow dish. Pour lemon juice over chicken. Cover and refrigerate for 2 to 3 hours.

- Remove chicken from juice and rub with oil. Combine remaining ingredients and stir well. Sprinkle seasonings on chicken.

- Place chicken skin side up on a moderate grill (350 to 375 degrees). Cook until done, turning every 20 minutes, about 60 to 80 minutes.

Serves: 4

Fresh Herb Grilled Chicken

Preparation Time: 15 minutes plus refrigeration time
Cook Time: 20 minutes

4	large whole chicken breasts, halved	1	tablespoon fresh tarragon, chopped
¾	cup olive oil	1	tablespoon fresh sage, chopped
¾	cup fresh lemon juice	1	tablespoon fresh oregano, chopped
1	teaspoon Dijon mustard	1	tablespoon fresh chives, chopped
4	cloves garlic, crushed	½	teaspoon salt
½	cup fresh parsley, chopped		Freshly ground pepper, to taste
1	tablespoon fresh rosemary, chopped		

- At least 2 hours before cooking, place chicken in a 9 x 13-inch pan. Combine remaining ingredients; pour over chicken. Marinate in refrigerator at least 2 hours.

- When ready to cook, drain chicken, reserving marinade. Grill chicken, brushing frequently with marinade, about 10 minutes per side or until done. Discard remaining marinade.

Serves: 8

North Carolina Chicken

Preparation Time: 10 minutes ~ Cook Time: 1 hour

2	cups bread crumbs	2	teaspoons salt
¾	cup Parmesan cheese, grated	¼	teaspoon pepper
¼	cup parsley, chopped	1	chicken, cut in pieces
1	clove garlic, pressed or minced	½	cup butter, melted

- Mix bread crumbs, cheese, parsley, garlic, salt, and pepper. Dip chicken pieces into melted butter, then into crumb mixture until coated well.

- Arrange pieces in an open shallow baking dish. Pour remaining butter over coated chicken and bake at 350 degrees for 1 hour. Baste frequently.

Serves: 4 to 6

Poppy Seed Chicken

Preparation Time: 15 minutes ~ Cook Time: 30 to 45 minutes

2	pounds boneless cooked chicken breasts cut into pieces	1½	cups butter crackers
1	10¾-ounce can cream of chicken soup	1	tablespoon poppy seeds
1	8-ounce container sour cream	½	cup butter or margarine

- Place chicken pieces in bottom of a 2-quart casserole dish. Mix together soup and sour cream. Pour over chicken.

- Melt butter and add poppy seeds and cracker crumbs. Mix well and place over the casserole. Bake at 350 degrees for 30 to 45 minutes.

Serves: 4

This recipe can be made ahead. Add the crumb mixture just before baking.

Oven Crispy Chicken

Preparation Time: 20 minutes ~ Cook Time: 45 to 60 minutes

1 8-ounce container "light" sour cream (may use regular; non-fat sour cream gives a different taste)	½ teaspoon salt
2 tablespoons fresh lemon juice	¼ teaspoon pepper
2 teaspoons Worcestershire sauce	8 boneless, skinless chicken breast halves (washed, patted dry) or breast halves with bones in
1 teaspoon paprika	3 cups cornmeal stuffing mix, crushed to a fine consistency
1 teaspoon celery salt	¼ cup butter, melted
½ teaspoon garlic salt	

- Combine sour cream, lemon juice, Worcestershire, paprika, celery salt, garlic salt, salt, and pepper. Dip chicken breasts first into sour cream mixture, then dredge in cornmeal crumbs.

- Place chicken in a lightly greased glass, ovenproof baking dish. Drizzle melted butter over chicken. Bake, uncovered, at 350 degrees for 45 minutes to 1 hour or until chicken is tender and crusty brown.

Serves: 8

Cornish Hens with Rosemary

Preparation Time: 15 minutes ~ Cook Time: 1 hour

4 Cornish game hens	2 teaspoons dried rosemary
8 cloves garlic, peeled	1 cup butter, melted
1 teaspoon salt	4 sprigs fresh rosemary, garnish
1 teaspoon pepper	

- Wash and pat dry hens. Place them in a shallow baking dish, loosen the skin and put 1 garlic clove under the breast skin of each hen and 1 garlic clove into cavity.

- Season with salt and pepper. Sprinkle dried rosemary over each hen. Pour melted butter over all the game hens. Bake at 350 degrees for 1 hour, basting every 15 minutes.

- Serve with garnish of fresh rosemary sprigs.

Serves: 4

Pineapple Chicken

Preparation Time: 20 minutes
Cook Time: 45 minutes

1	2 to 3-pound chicken, cut up
1	tablespoon sesame seeds
2	tablespoons vegetable oil
¼	cup sugar
2	tablespoons cornstarch
⅛	teaspoon ground ginger

1	15¼-ounce can crushed pineapple (not drained)
1	cup water
⅓	cup soy sauce
1	clove garlic, crushed

- Brown chicken and sesame seeds in oil in a large skillet.

- Combine sugar, cornstarch, and ginger in a medium saucepan. Mix well. Add pineapple, water, soy sauce, and garlic and cook over medium heat, stirring constantly until thick and bubbly.

- Pour sauce over chicken. Cover and simmer 45 minutes or until tender.

Serves: 6

Cranberry Chicken

Preparation Time: 10 minutes
Cook Time: 50 to 60 minutes

6	chicken breasts
1	16-ounce can whole cranberry sauce

1	8-ounce bottle Catalina dressing (may use reduced calorie)
1	package dried onion soup

- Put chicken in an 11 x 7-inch baking dish sprayed with cooking oil. Mix remaining ingredients together and pour over chicken.

- Bake, uncovered, at 350 degrees for 50 to 60 minutes.

Serves: 6

Variation: May substitute 12 ounces apricot jam for cranberry sauce. You can also substitute pork chops for chicken.

Rosemary-Smoked Turkey Breast

Preparation Time: 15 minutes
Cook Time: 45 to 60 minutes on gas grill or kettle grill

1	6-6½-pound turkey breast, boned	Salt and pepper
3-4	garlic cloves, sliced very thin	8-12 sprigs of fresh rosemary, approximately 6 inches long, soaked in water
1-2	tablespoons olive oil	

- Rinse turkey breast in cold water and pat dry. Loosen the skin and place the garlic slices over the breast in-between the meat and the skin. Coat skin with olive oil, then sprinkle with salt and pepper.

- Heat coals on one side of a gas grill or kettle grill to white-hot. Place the breast skin-side down over the coals, uncovered, to sear for 5 minutes. Slide turkey to the other side of the grill, off of the coals and place ½ of the rosemary on top of the turkey and beside it. Cover with grill lid, all vents open. Smoke for 20 minutes.

- Turn turkey over and add the rest of the rosemary. Cover and smoke for another 20 to 25 minutes. Remove from grill and let rest for 10 minutes. Carve in slices.

Serves: 8 to 10

Sesame Chicken

Preparation Time: 15 minutes   ~   Cook Time: 45 to 55 minutes

1   cup crushed soda crackers
     (use a food processor, about 20 to
     25 crackers depending on the size)
1   cup Parmesan cheese, freshly grated
2   tablespoons scallions (green and white
     parts), minced
2   tablespoons fresh parsley, chopped

½   teaspoon paprika
     Salt and freshly ground pepper, to taste
8   chicken thighs with skin or 1 whole
     chicken cut up
1   stick butter, melted
2   tablespoons sesame seeds, lightly toasted
     Softened butter

- Preheat oven to 375 degrees. Lightly spray a shallow 9 x 14-inch baking pan with cooking spray.

- In small bowl, mix cracker crumbs, Parmesan, scallions, parsley, paprika, salt, and pepper. Dip chicken in butter and roll each piece in cracker mixture to form thick coating.

- Arrange chicken pieces in single layer in baking pan. Sprinkle with sesame seeds and drizzle with remaining butter, if any, or dot with softened butter.

- Bake at 375 degrees for 45 to 55 minutes or until tender and golden. Serve hot, room temperature, or chilled.

Serves: 4

 When using glass ovenware, reduce the oven temperature by 25 degrees.

Sunday Roast Chicken

Preparation Time: 30 minutes ~ Cook Time: 3 to 4 hours

2 tablespoons butter or cooking spray	2 garlic cloves
2 cups onion, chopped	1 lemon, halved
1 pound package small carrots	Salt
1 teaspoon dried thyme	Pepper
½-1 cup white wine or water	Paprika
1 6 to 8-pound roasting chicken	

- In a large skillet with cooking spray or butter, sauté the onions, carrots, and thyme on medium heat for 10 minutes. Place vegetables in the bottom of a large roasting pan. Deglaze the skillet with the wine and pour over vegetables in the pan.

- While vegetables are cooking, rinse the chicken with cold water and pat dry. Salt the cavity and stuff with the garlic cloves and the lemon halves. Salt and pepper the outside of the chicken and dust evenly with paprika.

- Roast at 325 degrees for 3 to 4 hours. Baste every 15 minutes until chicken is done and the skin is mahogany brown. Serve the chicken and vegetables with the broth over rice.

Serves: 6 to 8

You can easily feed a crowd by roasting 2 or 3 chickens at the same time!

Tangy Chicken

Preparation Time: 10 minutes ~ Cook Time: 1 hour
May prepare ahead.

4 chicken breasts	½ teaspoon thyme
¼ cup butter or margarine, melted	¼ cup cider vinegar
1 teaspoon garlic salt	¼ cup lemon juice
1 teaspoon onion salt	Paprika
½ teaspoon black pepper	

- Place chicken breasts in a 13 x 9-inch baking dish.

- Melt butter in a small saucepan, add other ingredients, except paprika and stir well until blended.

- Pour sauce over chicken breasts and sprinkle with paprika. Cover the dish with foil and bake at 350 degrees for 1 hour.

Serves: 4

This is good with rice. Place breast on a bed of rice and pour sauce over it.
This simple sauce tastes like you have slaved over it for hours, so don't mention
the words, "easy," "simple," or "quick." Just smile and rake in the compliments.

Wine-Glazed Chicken and Vegetables

Preparation Time: 15 minutes ~ Cook Time: 1 hour

1	broiler or fryer, cut up		2	tablespoons lemon juice
1	teaspoon Accent		1	4-ounce can mushrooms, reserving liquid for divided use
½	teaspoon salt			
¼	teaspoon pepper		½	cup chicken broth
¼	cup corn oil		½	cup burgundy wine
2	tablespoons flour		12	small white onions, peeled (may use frozen)
1	teaspoon sugar			
⅛	teaspoon dried thyme		1	pound baby carrots
⅛	teaspoon dried rosemary			Parsley

- Sprinkle chicken with Accent, salt, and pepper. Heat oil in Dutch oven on medium heat. Add chicken. Brown lightly on all sides. Remove chicken.

- Mix flour, sugar, thyme, and rosemary. Stir into pan drippings to make a smooth paste. Add lemon juice, mushroom liquid, and broth. Cook, stirring, until it boils. Add wine, onions, carrots, mushrooms, and chicken.

- Reduce heat, cover, and simmer 30 minutes. Remove cover; continue cooking at a higher temperature until most of the liquid has evaporated and chicken and vegetables are coated. Garnish with parsley.

Serves: 4

Best Easy Brisket

Preparation Time: 5 minutes
Cook Time: 3 hours

1 box (2 packages) Campbell's dried onion soup mix	1 beef brisket (not corned beef), about 2 pounds, trimmed of fat
	1 can beer

- Sprinkle 1 packet of soup into a large skillet or shallow casserole with a tight-fitting lid. Put the brisket on top and sprinkle the other packet of soup over the meat.

- Pour ½ to ⅔ of the can of beer around the roast (don't rinse the soup off the meat). Cover tightly and cook at 300 degrees for 3 hours.

Serves: 6

Put this in the oven when you leave to pick the children up from school and by the time you've finished dance lessons and soccer practice, your dinner will be ready!

Company Beef Stew

Cook Time: 10 to 12 hours or 4 to 6 hours, depending on setting

Crock pot	1-2 bay leaves
2 pounds stew beef	1 teaspoon paprika
¼ cup flour	4 sliced carrots
1½ teaspoons salt	6 medium potatoes, diced
½-1 teaspoon fresh ground pepper	2 onions, chopped
1½ cups beef broth (or chicken broth)	2 stalks celery, sliced
1 teaspoon Worcestershire sauce	1 9-ounce package frozen peas
1 clove garlic, pressed or minced finely	

- Put meat and flour in crock pot with salt and pepper. Stir. Add all other ingredients, except peas. Add peas in the last 20 minutes.

- Cook on low setting 10 to 12 hours or on high setting 4 to 6 hours.

Serves: 4 to 6

Beef Stroganoff

Preparation Time: 15 minutes
Cook Time: 1 hour and 15 minutes

½	cup onion, chopped		1½	tablespoons lemon juice
¼	cup green pepper, chopped		1	4.5-ounce jar of sliced mushrooms, drained or 4 ounces fresh mushrooms, quartered
	Butter			
1-1½ pounds top round steak, cut in ¼-inch strips			1	8-ounce package wide egg noodles
	Salt and pepper		½	cup Burgundy wine
1	10.5-ounce can beef broth or consommé		1	cup sour cream (can add more, if you like)
¼	teaspoon garlic powder			

- In a large saucepan, sauté onions and peppers in butter. Add beef strips and sprinkle with salt and pepper. Brown.

- Add beef broth, garlic powder, lemon juice, and mushrooms. Cover and cook over low heat for 1 hour. If liquid is gone, add ¼ can beef broth and cook for 5 minutes longer.

- Meanwhile, cook egg noodles according to package. Time this so your noodles will be ready when the meat is done. Drain noodles and add to meat mixture. Add wine. Stir, cover, and simmer 10 minutes longer.

- Add sour cream, stir well, and simmer covered 5 minutes longer. Be careful not to boil.

Serves: 4 to 6

Chinese Lo Mein

Preparation Time: 30 minutes ~ Cook Time: 20 minutes

½-1 pound flank steak, sliced thinly across the grain

2 tablespoons soy sauce

2 tablespoons sherry

1 teaspoon sugar

1 teaspoon cornstarch

3 packages ramen noodles without the flavor packets

Olive oil for stir frying

1 onion, chopped

2 stalks celery, sliced

1 4-ounce can mushrooms

1 8-ounce can bamboo shoots

1 10-ounce package frozen peas, thawed

- Marinate sliced steak in mixture of soy sauce, sherry, sugar, and cornstarch for at least 15 minutes.

- Cook noodles for 3 minutes in boiling water. Drain and rinse with cold water. Set aside.

- In a large frying pan or wok over medium-high heat, fry steak in oil for 2 to 3 minutes until brown. Set aside.

- Stir-fry onions and celery for 3 minutes. Add mushrooms, bamboo shoots, peas, and steak. Add a little soy sauce and stir-fry. Set aside.

- Stir-fry noodles in oil. Add soy sauce to brown. Serve meat and vegetable mixture over noodles.

Serves: 5

Creamy Beef Stew

Preparation Time: 30 minutes ~ Cook Time: 2½ to 3 hours

Flour for dredging

Salt and pepper

2½ pounds stew beef, cut into ½ to 1 inch chunks

¼ cup canola or safflower oil, plus

2 cups onion, chopped

2 cloves garlic, pressed or minced

1 bay leaf

1½ cups red wine

Water or beef broth

2 teaspoons salt

1 pound carrots, baby or cut into 1-inch pieces

5 medium Yukon gold potatoes, cut into eighths

1½ cups sour cream
(you may use "light", but not "fat-free")

- Season flour with salt and pepper. Dredge beef in flour.

- Heat 2 tablespoons of oil in a large stew pot or Dutch oven over medium-high heat. Brown stew beef in batches in the hot oil. Add oil a couple of tablespoons at a time, as needed.

- When all the beef is browned, add the onion, garlic, bay leaf, wine, and enough water or beef broth to cover. Bring to a boil, cover, and reduce the heat to medium-low. Simmer for 1½ hours.

- Add salt, carrots, and potatoes. Add more liquid, if necessary, to just cover. Replace lid and simmer for another 1 to 1½ hours until beef is tender.

- Whisk in the sour cream. Season with extra salt and pepper, to taste. Do not boil.

Serves: 6

Deep Dish Steak Pie

Preparation Time: 10 to 15 minutes ~ Cook Time: 1 hour
Freezes well without the crust.

Single pie crust	¼ cup butter
1½ pounds stew beef	2 potatoes, peeled and sliced (or cubed)
¼ cup oil	2 carrots, thinly sliced
½ cup beef broth	1 onion, chopped
¼ cup white wine	⅓ cup flour
1 clove garlic, minced or pressed	1 cup half-and-half
1 teaspoon dried marjoram	1 cup frozen peas
1 bay leaf	1 egg, beaten
Salt and pepper, to taste	

- Prepare pie crust. Set aside.

- Brown meat in oil over medium-high heat. Stir in broth, wine, garlic, and seasonings. Bring to a boil. Reduce heat, cover, and simmer for 10 minutes.

- In a large saucepan, melt butter. Add potatoes, carrots, and onion and cook until tender, but not brown. Stir in flour. Add half-and-half, cook, and stir until thick and bubbly. Stir in the meat mixture, add the peas, and heat through.

- Transfer the mixture to a 2-quart casserole; place pie crust on top. Prick crust to vent. Turn pastry edge under and stick to side of casserole. Brush with beaten egg. Bake at 400 degrees for about 30 minutes until crust is golden.

Serves: 6

Can be frozen before adding the pie crust.

Flank Steak Teriyaki

Preparation Time: 5 minutes plus 4 hours marinating time
Cook Time: 10 to 15 minutes

¾ cup vegetable oil	2 tablespoons scallions, finely chopped
¼ cup soy sauce	1 large clove garlic, minced or pressed
¼ cup honey	½ teaspoon ground ginger
2 tablespoons vinegar	Flank steak

- Combine ingredients and pour over steak. Refrigerate for 4 hours or more, turning occasionally.

- Broil under high heat, 2 inches from burner or grill over white-hot coals, turning once, until done as desired (5 minutes per side for medium-rare).

- Let rest 10 minutes before carving across the grain into thin slices.

Serves: 6 to 8

Marinated London Broil

Preparation Time: 15 minutes plus marinating time
Cook Time: 15 to 20 minutes

½ cup ketchup	2 tablespoons white vinegar
1 teaspoon salt	2 tablespoons Worcestershire sauce
2 tablespoons steak sauce	2 tablespoons vegetable oil
2 tablespoons sugar	1½-2 pounds London broil

- Heat ketchup, salt, steak sauce, sugar, vinegar, Worcestershire sauce, and oil to boiling, stirring until thoroughly combined. Let cool to lukewarm.

- Pour marinade over London broil. Marinate in the refrigerator overnight, turning meat several times. Drain and discard marinade.

- Cook over medium coals or medium flame on the grill. Cook slowly to avoid charring. Let rest 10 to 15 minutes before slicing thinly across the grain.

Serves: 4 to 6

Meat or Poultry Marinade

1	tablespoon black peppercorns	6	ounces honey
4	tablespoons light brown sugar	½	cup soy sauce
5-6	cloves garlic	1	tablespoon Dijon mustard
1	teaspoon ground ginger	1½	cups olive oil

- Mix peppercorns, brown sugar, and garlic in a food processor or blender.

- Add the ginger, honey, soy sauce, mustard, and olive oil and mix well.

Yield: Makes enough marinade for 3 to 4 pounds of poultry, pork, or beef.

Marinated Beef Tenderloin

Preparation Time: 30 minutes plus marinating time
Cook Time: 45 to 60 minutes

1	cup port wine	½	teaspoon hot sauce
1	cup soy sauce	4	cloves garlic, crushed
½	cup olive oil	1	bay leaf
1	teaspoon pepper	1	5 to 6-pound beef tenderloin, trimmed
1	teaspoon whole dried thyme		

- Combine first 8 ingredients, mixing well. Place beef in a large shallow dish, pouring the wine mixture over the top. Cover tightly. Refrigerate 8 hours; turning periodically.

- When ready to cook, drain off and reserve marinade and place beef on a rack in a pan. Insert a meat thermometer; do not touch fat.

- Bake at 425 degrees for 45 to 60 minutes or until thermometer registers 140 degrees for rare. Baste occasionally with marinade.

- Bake until thermometer registers 150 degrees for medium-rare, 160 degrees for medium. Let rest for 10 to 15 minutes before carving.

Serves: 12 generously

This is great as an appetizer or as an entrée!

Mexican Beef Pie

Preparation Time: 15 minutes ~ Cook Time: 30 to 35 minutes

1	pound ground beef	¼	cup water
¼	cup diced green chilies (4-ounce can)	1	8-ounce package corn muffin mix
1	14½-ounce can diced tomatoes	⅓	cup milk
⅔	cup frozen corn kernels (optional)	1	egg
1	tablespoon chili powder	2	cups Cheddar cheese, grated
½	teaspoon garlic powder		

- Brown ground beef in skillet. When beef is no longer pink, add green chilies, tomatoes, corn, chili powder, garlic, and water. Cook uncovered on medium heat for 5 minutes.

- In a medium bowl, combine corn muffin mix, milk, and egg. Coat a 9 x 13-inch baking dish with cooking spray. Spread corn muffin mixture over bottom of pan. Cover with ground beef mixture and sprinkle cheese over meat layer.

- Bake at 400 degrees for 30 to 35 minutes until bubbly and cheese is melted.

Serves: 6

Moving Day Casserole

Preparation Time: 25 minutes ~ Cook Time: 30 minutes

1	7-ounce box elbow macaroni	¼	teaspoon basil
1	pound extra lean ground beef		Dash garlic powder
1	15 to 18-ounce can tomato sauce		Dash pepper
1	15.25-ounce can niblet corn	1½	cups Cheddar cheese, grated
½	teaspoon Italian herbs	1½	cups Monterey Jack cheese, grated

- Cook macaroni. Drain. Set aside.

- In a large frying pan, brown ground beef. Drain. Add all the other ingredients to beef except for the cheeses.

- Place half of the meat and noodle mixture in the bottom of a casserole dish. Cover with Cheddar cheese. Add the rest of the beef/noodle mixture. Cover with Monterey Jack cheese.

- Bake at 350 degrees for 30 minutes or microwave on high for 10 minutes.

Serves: 8

Poor Boy Fillets

Preparation Time: 20 minutes plus refrigeration time of 2 hours
Cook Time: about 15 minutes

1	pound ground beef	3	tablespoons green pepper, finely chopped
1	4-ounce can mushroom pieces, drained	⅛	teaspoon salt
¼	cup Parmesan cheese, grated	½	teaspoon lemon pepper seasoning
3	tablespoons black olives, finely chopped	12	slices bacon
2	tablespoons onion, finely chopped		

- Shape ground beef into a 12 x 7½-inch rectangle on waxed paper. Sprinkle mushrooms, Parmesan, olives, onion, green pepper, salt, and lemon pepper evenly over beef.

- Begin at short end and roll like a jelly roll. Carefully slide roll onto jelly-roll pan, seam-side down. Cover and refrigerate 2 hours.

- Cook bacon until transparent (not crisp). Drain. Cut beef into 6 even slices. Wrap 2 pieces of bacon around edges of each fillet and secure with wooden picks.

- Grill fillets 4 to 5 inches from hot coals 8 minutes on each side, or to desired degree of doneness.

Serves: 6

Rapid Roast Beef

Preparation Time: 10 minutes
Cook Time: 2 hours and 30 minutes

5-6	pounds eye of round, prime rib, or boneless top sirloin beef roast	Garlic salt

- Preheat oven to 500 degrees. Rub meat on all surfaces with garlic salt. Place roast on broiler pan with rack. Put roast in preheated oven and roast for 30 to 33 minutes. Turn heat off, but do not open oven door. Leave roast in oven for 2 hours.

- 30 minutes cooking time yields a rare roast. 34 minutes cooking time will yield a medium-rare roast. Increase roasting time for more well-done meat. The outside is crusty and seasoned and the inside is juicy and tender.

Serves: 10 to 12

Mexican Salsa Beef

Preparation Time: 10 minutes
Cook Time: 2 hours

2 pounds London broil, cut into small,
   bite-sized pieces
1 tablespoon olive oil
1 medium jar salsa, about 16 ounces
2 tablespoons brown sugar

2 tablespoons soy sauce
2 cloves garlic, minced
2 tablespoons fresh lime juice
¼ cup coriander, chopped

- Brown meat in oil in Dutch oven over medium-high heat. Add salsa, sugar, soy, and garlic. Simmer, covered, 1½ hours.

- Uncover and simmer an additional 30 minutes. Add water, if necessary. Remove from heat, add lime juice and coriander. Serve over rice.

Serves: 4

Zesty Grilled Flank Steak

Preparation Time: 4 hours
Cook Time: 25 minutes

¾ cup vegetable oil
½ cup honey mustard
2 tablespoons red wine vinegar
2 tablespoons scallions, chopped

1 large clove garlic, chopped
1½ teaspoons ground ginger
1½ pounds flank steak

- Combine first 6 ingredients in a food processor or a blender to make the marinade. Pour over steak in a large ziploc bag or a glass baking dish. Marinate for at least 4 hours or overnight.

- Grill 7 minutes per side for medium-rare. Let rest for 10 minutes before carving across the grain of the meat.

Serves: 4

South-of-the-Border Pie

Preparation Time: 15 minutes ~ Cook Time: 55 to 60 minutes

1 pound lean ground beef
1 medium onion, finely chopped
1 package taco seasoning mix (1¼-ounces)
¾ cup water
1 16-ounce can refried beans
   (may use the fat-free variety)

1 8-ounce jar taco or picante sauce, divided use
1 baked 9-inch pastry shell
2 cups sharp Cheddar cheese, shredded
1 cup crushed corn chips
   Iceberg lettuce, shredded
1-2 tomatoes, chopped

- Cook ground beef and onion in a heavy skillet until meat is brown and crumbly in texture. Drain any fat from meat. Add taco seasoning mix and water, and then stir well to blend.

- Bring mixture to a boil. Reduce heat and simmer 20 minutes, stirring occasionally. Combine refried beans and ⅓ cup taco or picante sauce.

- Spoon ½ of the bean mixture into the bottom of the baked pie crust. Top with half of the meat mixture, half of the cheese, and all of the corn chips. Repeat layers: bean mixture, meat mixture, then cheese.

- Bake at 400 degrees for 20 to 25 minutes.

- Slice like a pie to serve. Spoon shredded lettuce and chopped tomatoes over pie slice. May choose taco sauce, salsa, and/or sour cream as an extra topping.

Serves: 6

Bourbon and Mustard-Glazed Pork Chops

Preparation Time: 5 minutes ~ Cook Time: 25 minutes

2 tablespoons Dijon mustard
2 tablespoons bourbon (or frozen orange juice concentrate)
2 tablespoons molasses
1 tablespoon light brown sugar

1 tablespoon vegetable oil
1 tablespoon soy sauce
¼ teaspoon fresh ground black pepper
4 pork loin chops, cut 1¼ inches thick

- Mix together all ingredients, except for chops. Place chops on an unheated broiler pan and broil 3 inches from heat for 12 minutes. Turn chops over and broil 12 to 14 minutes more, or until no pink remains.

- Brush chops with glaze throughout broiling process. Brush again with glaze before serving.

Serves: 4

May also be grilled and can be used on pork tenderloin.

Chinese Marinated Pork Tenderloins

Preparation Time: 10 minutes plus marinating time
Cook Time: 15 to 20 minutes

¼ cup soy sauce
3 tablespoons dry white wine
2 tablespoons fresh lemon juice
2 tablespoons oil
¾ teaspoon fine herbs
(parsley, chives, tarragon)

½ teaspoon gingerroot, grated
1 clove garlic, minced
¼ teaspoon onion powder
Dash pepper
2-3 pounds pork tenderloins

- Combine all marinade ingredients. Pour over tenderloins and marinate for 2 to 3 hours minimum, refrigerated.
- Grill 5 to 7 minutes per side or until done to your liking.

Serves: 6 to 8

Grilled Pork Tenderloins

Preparation Time: 15 minutes plus marinating time
Cook Time: 20 to 30 minutes

½ cup teriyaki sauce
½ cup soy sauce
3 tablespoons light brown sugar
1 clove garlic, pressed
1 tablespoon sesame seeds

½ teaspoon ground ginger
½ teaspoon pepper
1 tablespoon toasted sesame oil or
vegetable oil
3 1½-pound packages pork tenderloins

- Combine first 8 ingredients. Pour into a dish or a large ziplock bag and add pork tenderloins. Marinate for several hours or overnight in refrigerator.
- Grill until done (depends on size of tenderloins). Cut in ¼-inch medallions.

Serves: 8

Just~In~Thyme
Pork Tenderloin

Preparation Time: 10 minutes ~ Cook Time: 20 minutes

1	teaspoon salt	3	tablespoons dried thyme
½	teaspoon pepper	2	tablespoons olive oil or vegetable oil
½	teaspoon garlic powder	1½-2 pounds pork tenderloin	

- Combine dry ingredients. Rub pork with oil and sprinkle with dry ingredients on all sides.

- Grill pork on a hot grill (400 degrees) for 10 to 13 minutes per side, depending on desired degree of doneness.

Serves: 6

Pork Kebabs

Preparation Time: 30 minutes plus marinating time
Cook Time: 15 to 20 minutes.

1	8-ounce can crushed pineapple	3-3½ pounds boneless pork leg or shoulder, cut in 1½-inch cubes	
2	cloves garlic, cut in half		
1	teaspoon ginger	2	large red or green peppers, cut into 1½-inch squares
2	tablespoons red wine vinegar		
3	tablespoons soy sauce	1	large fresh pineapple, peeled, cored, and cut into 1½-inch cubes
½	cup hoisin sauce		
½	cup ketchup		

- Combine canned pineapple and its juice, garlic, ginger, vinegar, soy, hoisin, and ketchup in a large container with a lid. Add pork and stir to coat. Refrigerate overnight, stirring several times.

- On 8 metal skewers, thread meat alternately with bell peppers and pineapple. Grill on a lightly greased grill, basting often with leftover marinade. Turn frequently and cook 15 to 20 minutes or until meat is no longer pink in the center.

Serves: 8

This is a delicious prepare-ahead summer cookout with friends. Serve with corn-on-the-cob and a salad. Easy and wonderful.

Roast Pork
with Garlic and Herbs

Preparation Time: 10 minutes ~ Cook Time: 1 hour and 20 minutes.

6 large garlic cloves, pressed or minced finely	1 teaspoon pepper
5 teaspoons fresh rosemary, chopped	1 3-pound boneless pork loin
5 teaspoons parsley, chopped	½ cup heated apple juice may be added at the end to the juices, optional
2 teaspoons salt	

- Preheat oven to 400 degrees.

- Line a large roasting pan with foil. Mix first 5 ingredients in blender or food processor. Rub mixture all over the pork loin. Place pork fat-side down in pan.

- Roast 35 to 40 minutes, then turn fat-side up. Roast until meat thermometer registers 160 degrees, about 35 minutes longer. Remove from oven and let stand 10 minutes. Pour juices over roast and slice cross-wise.

Serves: 6 to 8

Herb-Garlic Crusted
Rack of Lamb

Preparation Time: 20 minutes ~ Cook Time: 30 minutes

2 racks of lamb, 8 to 9 ribs each	1 teaspoon kosher salt
2 tablespoons coarsely ground cornmeal	Freshly ground black pepper, to taste
2 teaspoons fresh rosemary, minced	3 tablespoons Dijon mustard
2 cloves garlic, minced	

- Cut racks in half. Preheat oven to 500 degrees. Combine the cornmeal, rosemary, garlic, salt, and pepper in a small bowl, mixing well.

- Lightly brush the fat side of the racks with the mustard. Place in oven for 10 minutes, braising the fat. Remove from oven and reduce temperature to 425 degrees.

- Quickly coat the mustard with the cornmeal mixture. Continue baking 20 more minutes for medium-rare. Slice the chops apart and serve immediately.

Serves: 4

Foolproof Grilled Leg of Lamb

Preparation Time: 3 hours and 30 minutes ~ Cook Time: 50 to 60 minutes

1	4 to 5-pound leg of lamb, boned and butterflied (get your butcher to do this)
1	small onion, sliced thin
2	cloves garlic, sliced
	Juice of 1 lemon
½	cup red wine vinegar
¾	cup safflower or canola oil
¼	teaspoon dried oregano or ¾ teaspoon fresh oregano

¼	teaspoon dried thyme or ¾ teaspoon fresh thyme
½	teaspoon dried rosemary or ¾ teaspoon fresh rosemary
½	teaspoon dried basil or ¾ teaspoon fresh basil
1	teaspoon salt
	Dash pepper

- Place lamb, flattened, in a glass casserole dish just large enough to hold it.

- Combine remaining ingredients and pour over meat. Marinate at least 3 hours in the refrigerator, turning occasionally.

- Roast meat over a very hot charcoal fire for 25 to 30 minutes per side for medium-rare. Let "rest" at least 10 minutes after grilling, before carving.

Serves: 6 to 8

This is especially good with garlic mashed potatoes, sautéed baby asparagus, and an Australian Shiraz red wine.

Marinated Leg of Lamb

Preparation Time: 10 minutes plus marinating time of 12 hours
Cook Time: 1 hour and 15 minutes to 1 hour and 35 minutes

1	6-pound leg of lamb, fat trimmed	½	teaspoon pepper
1	tablespoon lemon juice	1	teaspoon oregano
2	tablespoons red wine vinegar	1	teaspoon basil
1	teaspoon salt	1	large onion, chopped

- Combine all ingredients and marinate lamb at least 12 hours, refrigerated.

- Preheat oven to 350 degrees and place lamb in a roasting pan. Roast until an instant-read thermometer inserted into the thickest part of the meat reads 120 to 125 degrees for medium-rare; 135 to 140 degrees for medium. Cooking time will be between 10 to 15 minutes per pound.

- Remove from oven and let rest 15 to 20 minutes before carving.

Serves: 6 to 8

Veal Marsala

Preparation Time: 30 minutes
Cook Time: 1 hour

2	pounds veal slices, pounded thin	½	pound mushrooms, sliced
	Flour	2	cloves fresh garlic, pressed or minced
2	tablespoons butter	⅔	cup Marsala wine
2	tablespoons olive oil	3	tablespoons Parmesan cheese, grated

- Cut veal into bite-sized pieces. Dredge in flour. Brown in butter and olive oil over medium-high heat.

- Transfer to a 9 x 13-inch covered baking dish. Add the remaining ingredients. Mix well.

- Cover and bake at 325 degrees for 45 minutes. Serve with long-grain and wild rice.

Serves: 4

May also be made with chicken breasts.

Roasted Leg of Lamb
à la Provence

Preparation Time: 20 minutes
Cook Time: about 1 hour and 30 minutes

6	whole heads of garlic	4	large sprigs of fresh rosemary
2½	tablespoons extra-virgin olive oil		Coarse salt and pepper
1	large bouquet garni: 4 sprigs of parsley, 4 sprigs of fresh thyme, and 2 bay leaves, fastened with butcher twine	1	leg of lamb, about 5 pounds, tied and trimmed of fat (ask your butcher to do this for you)

- Slice off the top third of each head of garlic. Place in the roasting pan, cut-side up. Drizzle with olive oil. Place the bouquet garni in the middle and place the rosemary around the garlic.

- Put a small metal roasting rack on top of the garlic and herbs. Season the lamb well with salt and pepper and place on the metal rack.

- Roast in the oven at 425 degrees for 10 to 12 minutes per pound for medium-rare and 15 minutes per pound for medium. Turn the lamb several times during the roasting and baste occasionally.

- Remove the lamb from the oven and roasting pan and let rest on a carving board for 20 to 25 minutes. Tent with foil while resting. Meanwhile, place the garlic on a large serving platter; cover and keep warm in a low oven.

- Place the roasting pan over medium heat and scrape up any bits from the bottom. Cook for a couple of minutes, scraping and stirring until nearly caramelized. Spoon off excess fat. Add ¼ cup cold water, bring to a boil, turn heat to low, and simmer about 5 minutes. Strain the sauce through a sieve and pour into a gravy boat.

- Carve the lamb into thin slices. Place on the warmed serving platter surrounded by the garlic.

Serves: 6 to 8

Veal Scaloppini

Preparation Time: 20 minutes
Cook Time: about 50 minutes

12	slices veal scallops	1-2	cloves garlic, minced or pressed
	Flour for dredging	1	chicken bouillon cube dissolved in cup
	Salt and pepper, to taste		warm water, or 1 cup chicken broth
2	tablespoons butter	10-15	mushrooms, sliced
2	tablespoons olive oil	½	cup dry white wine
¾	cup onion, chopped finely		

- Dust veal lightly with flour and season with salt and pepper. Veal may be pounded if you prefer the slices to be thinner.

- Heat butter and oil in skillet until hot, but not smoking. Brown veal slices on both sides and remove to a heated platter. Reduce heat to medium and add onion and garlic and cook until onions are soft and clear, stirring frequently. Add more oil if necessary when cooking the onions and garlic.

- Add chicken broth. Scrape the bottom of the pan. Add the mushrooms and bring to a boil.

- Add the veal slices and simmer for about 10 to 15 minutes. Add the wine and simmer for another 10 minutes until the liquid is reduced and thickened.

Serves: 6

To make Steak Diane, substitute ½-inch thin beef tenderloin slices for the veal, beef broth for the chicken broth, and red wine for the white wine.

Crab Imperial

Preparation Time: 30 minutes
Cook Time: 25 to 30 minutes

1	egg, slightly beaten		1	teaspoon horseradish
1-1½	tablespoons mayonnaise		¼	teaspoon Old Bay seasoning
	(start with 1 tablespoon)		½	teaspoon lemon juice
2	teaspoons dry mustard		½	teaspoon salt
1	teaspoon Worcestershire sauce		½	teaspoon pepper
1	4-ounce jar chopped pimentos		1	pound fresh back fin crabmeat (not
½	teaspoon hot sauce			frozen), picked through for shells
1	tablespoon green pepper, finely chopped			

- Mix egg, mayonnaise, then all the other ingredients, gently adding the crab last. (May refrigerate 3 to 5 hours to enhance flavors prior to cooking.)

- Place mixture in individual 4-ounce baking dishes, or crab shells. Bake at 350 degrees for 25 to 30 minutes.

Serves: 4 to 6

Imperial mixture may also be used to stuff mushroom caps or large shrimp for appetizers, or stuffed shrimp as an entrée.

Crab Cakes for the Purist

Preparation Time: 20 minutes plus 1 hour refrigeration time
Cook Time: 10 minutes

1	pound back fin crabmeat	2	teaspoons dry mustard
1	egg	1	tablespoon mayonnaise
1	teaspoon fresh parsley, chopped	10-12	club or captain's crackers, crushed
1	teaspoon horseradish (more if you like)		Olive oil, enough to cover the bottom of a frying pan
½	teaspoon hot sauce		

- Pick through crabmeat, removing any shells. Combine egg, parsley, horseradish, hot sauce, mustard, and mayonnaise, and gently toss the mixture with the crabmeat, trying not to break up the crab chunks.

- Shape into 4 to 6 balls and roll gently in the cracker crumbs. Refrigerate at least 1 hour before cooking.

- Heat a frying pan with olive oil (barely cover the bottom) on medium heat.

- Sauté the crab cakes on medium-high heat until golden brown, pressing lightly with a spatula to form the "cakes". Flip and cook other side until golden brown. Serve immediately.

Serves: 4 to 6

In our family, summer is marked by the crab-not a real one-but the electric, red neon crab that glows in the window of Mrs. Simpson's Crab House in Wilmington, NC.

Mrs. Simpson, a warm, sweet woman with a shy demeanor, usually opens her shop in mid-May, but you can never be certain until the neon crab is lit. Little old ladies sit for hours carefully picking the crabs to make our favorite summer staple possible. We eagerly await the delicate back fin meat for the summer's crab cakes. The end of the season is marked by my father's Seafood Cornucopia Stew, which includes the last of Mrs. Simpson's crab. She closes her shop the night before Thanksgiving. The stew is as much a Thanksgiving ritual as crabmeat is to our summer.

Seared Tuna
Pepper Steaks

Preparation Time: 10 minutes ~ Cook Time: 20 minutes

2¼ teaspoons cracked black pepper
2   tuna steaks, 1¼ inches thick
     Salt
2   teaspoons olive oil

¼   cup unsalted butter
½   teaspoon dried sage
¼   cup low-sodium chicken broth, canned
½   cup brandy

- Press cracked pepper onto each side of each tuna steak and sprinkle lightly with salt.

- Heat a heavy skillet to medium-high and add olive oil. Add tuna to skillet and sear until cooked to desired doneness, about 3½ minutes per side for medium. Transfer tuna to plates. Tent with foil to keep warm.

- Add butter and sage to skillet. Heat over medium heat until butter is melted. Remove from heat. Add broth, then brandy.

- Place skillet over high heat and boil until sauce is reduced to ⅓ cup. Season with salt and pepper. Spoon over tuna.

Serves: 2

Salmon Supreme

Preparation Time: 15 minutes
Cook Time: 10 to 15 minutes

4	tablespoons butter, melted	1	teaspoon Dijon mustard
3	tablespoons fresh lemon juice	1	teaspoon dried tarragon, or 1 tablespoon fresh tarragon
1	teaspoon Worcestershire sauce		
½	teaspoon kosher salt	1	tablespoon fresh parsley, chopped
¼	teaspoon paprika	4	8-ounce center cut salmon fillets, skinned
¼	teaspoon freshly ground black pepper		Garlic salt

- Combine butter, lemon juice, Worcestershire sauce, salt, paprika, pepper, mustard, tarragon, and parsley in a glass baking dish large enough to accommodate the salmon fillets.

- Place fillets in marinade, turning to coat evenly. Let salmon marinate while oven is preheating or while preparing grill. Sprinkle lightly with garlic salt.

- Bake salmon at 400 degrees for 15 minutes or until fish flakes with fork and is no longer translucent in center, or grill 4 to 5 minutes per side basting until done.

Serves: 4 to 6

Lime-Seasoned Salmon

Preparation Time: 10 minutes plus marinating time
Cook Time: 12 minutes

¼	cup salad oil	2	teaspoons toasted sesame oil
¼	cup lime juice	2	teaspoons honey
1	tablespoon water	4	salmon steaks, 6 ounces each and about 1½ to 2 inches thick
1	tablespoon soy sauce		

- Mix oil, lime juice, water, soy sauce, sesame oil, and honey. Place salmon in a plastic ziplock bag and add the marinade. Refrigerate 8 to 24 hours, turning occasionally.

- Grill over medium hot coals for 6 minutes per side.

Serves: 4

Salmon and Leek En Croûte with Chile Cream Sauce

Preparation Time: 45 minutes plus at least 1 hour refrigeration
Cook Time: 30 minutes

Salmon

4	large leeks	¼	teaspoon white pepper
2	tablespoons unsalted butter	1	large egg
2¼	pounds skinless, salmon fillet	1	tablespoon water
1	teaspoon lime zest, freshly grated	1	17.25-ounce package frozen puff pastry sheets, thawed
¼	cup fresh dill leaves, chopped		
½	teaspoon kosher salt		

Cream Sauce

1	jar 4 to 5 roasted red pepper pieces	1	cup sour cream
1	teaspoon red or green hot chili, seeded and minced	1	cup crème fraîche

- Cut leeks crosswise into ½-inch slices. Wash thoroughly and pat dry. Sauté in a large skillet in the butter over medium-high heat until tender. Cool.

- Cut salmon into ¾-inch pieces, toss with leeks, lime zest, dill, salt, and pepper in a bowl. Set aside.

- In a small bowl, make an egg wash with the egg and water.

- On a lightly floured surface, roll 1 puff pastry sheet into a 10-inch square and the other sheet into a 12-inch square.

- Transfer the 10-inch square to a floured baking sheet and pile salmon mixture into a 9-inch circular mound in the center, leaving a margin all the way around. Brush the margin with the egg wash.

- Place the remaining pastry square over the salmon and press the edges to seal. Trim to a 10-inch circumference. Crimp edges and cut 4 steam vents on top of crust. Brush with egg wash. Chill pie at least 1 hour. Bake in a preheated 400-degree oven for 30 minutes.

- For the sauce, use a blender or food processor to blend pepper pieces, chili, sour cream, and crème fraîche until smooth. Serve chilled with the salmon.

Serves: 6

This can be made ahead and refrigerated until ready to bake. Elegant and delicious!

Sautéed Flounder with Capers

Preparation Time: 10 minutes ~ Cook Time: 8 to 12 minutes

4 large flounder fillets	1-2 tablespoons olive oil
1 cup flour, seasoned with salt and pepper	½ 3.5-ounce bottle small capers
1 teaspoon Old Bay seasoning	1-2 tablespoons fresh lemon juice
3 tablespoons butter, divided use	

- Wash fillets, removing any bones in neck area. Pat dry. Combine flour and Old Bay. Dust fillets in flour mixture.

- Melt 2 tablespoons butter with olive oil over medium heat in black cast iron pan or heavy skillet. Cook fillets 4 to 6 minutes each side. Remove fillets.

- Add remaining tablespoon butter to pan, add capers and lemon juice, heating thoroughly. Pour over fish and serve immediately.

Serves: 4

Parmesan Flounder

Preparation Time: 15 minutes ~ Cook Time: 7 minutes

4 flounder or catfish fillets, 4 to 6 ounces each	3 tablespoons Parmesan cheese, grated
Vegetable cooking spray	1 tablespoon scallions, finely chopped
1 tablespoon fresh lemon juice	1 tablespoon butter, softened
¼ cup mayonnaise (not salad dressing)	⅛ teaspoon Texas Pete or other hot sauce

- Place the fillets on a broiler pan coated with cooking spray and brush lemon juice onto fillets. Broil 5 to 6 inches from heat with the oven door partially open for 5 to 6 minutes or until fish flakes easily.

- Combine the mayonnaise, Parmesan cheese, scallions, butter, and hot sauce. Whisk to mix very thoroughly. Spread the mixture evenly over the fillets.

- Broil 1 additional minute or until lightly browned and bubbly. Do not overcook!

Serves: 4

The mayonnaise mixture can be made ahead of time and refrigerated.

White Bean
and Shrimp Gumbo

PreparationTime: Soak beans overnight ~ Cook Time: about 5 hours

1   cup dry white beans, soaked overnight in cold water, drained

½   pound hot sausage: Italian, andouille, or kielbasa

¼   cup olive oil

⅓   cup flour

1   cup onions, chopped

½   cup bell pepper, chopped

1   cup okra, chopped

1   cup parsley, chopped

1   cup scallions, chopped

1   teaspoon garlic, minced or pressed

2   cups dry white wine

2   tablespoons Worcestershire sauce

1   teaspoon celery seed
     Salt, to taste
     Tabasco sauce, to taste

1½   pounds shrimp, shelled and deveined

- Put the beans and sausage in a medium saucepan and cover with water. Bring to a boil, reduce heat, cover, and simmer, adding water as necessary and stirring until beans are cooked, about 1½ hours.

- Meanwhile, put oil in a large heavy pot. Heat over very low heat until hot. Add flour and stir with a whisk almost constantly until cooked to a dark brown, but be careful not to burn. This is a slow process and will take at least 25 minutes.

- Raise heat to medium-low and add onion, bell pepper, okra, parsley, and scallions. Cook 5 minutes. Add garlic and ½ cup water. Cook 5 more minutes. Add enough water to cover by 2 inches.

- Drain cooked beans. Reserve sausage. Puree beans in blender or food processor. Add to onion mixture along with wine, Worcestershire sauce, celery seed, salt, and Tabasco. Cover with lid a little ajar. Over low heat, simmer, stirring often for about 3 hours.

- Taste and adjust seasoning. Slice sausage into ½-inch pieces. Add sausage and shrimp and cook until shrimp are just pink. Serve immediately over rice.

Serves: 6

Spiced Grilled Shrimp

Preparation Time: 1 hour plus marinating time
Cook Time: 6 minutes

2	pounds large shrimp, about 60	1	teaspoon ground white pepper
1	cup olive oil	1	teaspoon ground ginger
3	garlic cloves, peeled and minced	½	teaspoon ground cumin
1	tablespoon onion, grated	¼	teaspoon ground cloves
1	tablespoon sugar		Bamboo skewers
2	teaspoons salt		

- Peel and devein shrimp (may leave the tails on). Set aside in a container.
- Combine all remaining ingredients in a jar with a tight-fitting lid. Shake well. Add to shrimp and marinate 5 to 24 hours in refrigerator. Stir occasionally.
- Soak bamboo skewers in water. Put shrimp on skewers and grill or broil for 3 minutes per side. Serve immediately.

Serves: 6

Baked Snapper Greek Style

Preparation Time: 10 minutes ~ Cook Time: 45 minutes

2	pounds snapper fillets	1	garlic clove, chopped
1	tablespoon lemon juice	2	medium tomatoes, chopped
	Salt and fresh ground pepper, to taste	¾	cup parsley, finely chopped
	Pinch dried oregano	½	cup water
¼	cup olive oil	2	tablespoons dry bread crumbs
1	medium onion, chopped		Butter, softened

- Place fish in a well-greased baking dish. Sprinkle with lemon juice, salt, pepper, and oregano.
- Heat oil in a sauté pan over medium-high heat. Sauté onion until golden. Stir in garlic, tomatoes, parsley, and water.
- Pour mixture over fish and sprinkle with bread crumbs. Dot with butter and bake in a preheated 350 degree oven for 40 to 45 minutes, or until fish is tender.

Serves: 4

Shrimp and Scallops Gruyère

Preparation Time: 30 minutes ~ Cook Time: 30 minutes

¾ cup plus 1 tablespoon butter, divided use
¾ cup flour
3 cups milk, warmed
12 ounces Swiss Gruyère cheese, grated
¼ teaspoon garlic powder
Salt to taste
¼ teaspoon pepper
¼ teaspoon dry mustard

2 teaspoons tomato paste
3 teaspoons lemon juice, divided use
1 pound raw scallops
½ pound mushrooms, sliced
2 tablespoons green peppers, minced (optional)
1 pound cleaned shrimp

- In a 1-quart saucepan, melt ¾ cup butter over low heat. Whisk in the flour and cook for several minutes. Whisk in the milk and stir constantly until sauce is thickened.

- Add cheese to sauce and stir until melted. Add garlic powder, salt, pepper, mustard, tomato paste, and 2 teaspoons of the lemon juice. Leave on low heat.

- Meanwhile, poach scallops for 5 minutes with 1 teaspoon lemon juice and a dash of salt. Drain.

- Sauté mushrooms and peppers in remaining 2 tablespoons butter. Add to sauce. Add scallops and shrimp to cheese sauce. Heat over low heat for 10 to 15 minutes. Serve over rice.

Serves: 4 to 6

Sesame Grilled Fish

Preparation Time: 10 minutes plus 8 hours marinating time
Cook Time: 15 minutes

¼ cup orange juice
2 tablespoons ketchup
2 tablespoons soy sauce
1½ teaspoons lemon juice
¼ teaspoon pepper

2 tablespoons sesame oil
1 tablespoon brown sugar
1½ pounds fish, preferably grouper or salmon
1 tablespoon sesame seeds, toasted

- Combine first 7 ingredients and pour over fish. Marinate fish overnight.

- Grill over hot coals 15 minutes. Top with sesame seeds.

Serves: 4

Lime~Grilled Mahi~Mahi

Preparation Time: 1 hour ~ Cook Time: 12 to 15 minutes

⅓ cup olive oil (not extra-virgin)
⅓ cup dry white wine
   Juice of 2 limes
2 tablespoons parsley, chopped
1 teaspoon salt

1 teaspoon pepper
1 clove garlic, minced finely
4-6 mahi-mahi (or grouper) fillets, washed and patted dry

- Mix all ingredients except fish for marinade. Arrange fillets skin-side down in glass dish and pour marinade over. Refrigerate 30 to 40 minutes.

- Place fillets into a fillet basket coated with vegetable spray. Grill over the preheated medium setting of gas grill or charcoal grill skin-side down first, 5 to 6 minutes per side. For extra thick grouper, more cooking time may be needed. Do NOT overcook.

Serves: 4 to 6

Side Dishes and Vegetables

Singular to Versatile

Side Dishes and Vegetables

Sautéed Lemon Asparagus

Preparation Time: 10 minutes ~ Cook Time: 10 minutes

1	pound baby asparagus (very thin)	2	tablespoons fresh lemon juice
2	tablespoons butter	6	whole lemon slices, cut very thin
1	tablespoon olive oil		Dash salt

- Wash and trim asparagus.

- In a large frying pan, melt the butter over medium heat with the olive oil, then add the lemon juice. Reduce the heat to medium-low, add the asparagus, lemon slices, and salt.

- Toss to coat with butter. Cover and simmer for 5 to 8 minutes. Remove from heat and serve.

Serves: 6

Southwest Baked Beans

Preparation Time: 15 minutes ~ Cook Time: 1 hour and 30 minutes

---

1	15¼-ounce can red kidney beans	2	tablespoons honey
1	16-ounce can black beans	2	teaspoons oregano
1	19-ounce can cannellini beans	2	teaspoons dry mustard
1	28-ounce can diced tomatoes, drained	2	teaspoons cumin
1	cup onion, chopped	1½	teaspoons ginger
2	cloves garlic, chopped or pressed	1	teaspoon chili powder
¼	cup molasses		Pinch crushed red pepper flakes
¼	cup cider vinegar		

- Drain and rinse beans. Place in a 3-quart baking dish and add remaining ingredients.

- Mix gently and bake, covered, for 1½ hours at 350 degrees.

Serves: 8 to 10

Chilled Spiced Asparagus

Preparation Time: 15 to 20 minutes ~ Refrigerate for 3 or more hours

1 pound or 1 bunch of fresh thin asparagus, trimmed	½ teaspoon salt
⅓ cup vinegar	4 whole cloves
¼ cup water	¼ teaspoon celery seed
¼ cup sugar	1 stick cinnamon

- Blanch asparagus in boiling water until crisp-tender, 3 to 5 minutes. Plunge into ice water, drain and place in a shallow dish.

- Combine remaining ingredients in a small saucepan and cook over low heat until sugar has dissolved. Let cool.

- Pour over asparagus and marinate several hours or overnight.

- At serving time, remove from the marinade and serve on a platter or on individual plates.

Serves: 6

Even non-asparagus lovers love this one!

Lemon Broccoli

Preparation Time: 30 minutes ~ Cook Time: 10 minutes

2 tablespoons fresh lemon peel, grated	1½ pounds fresh broccoli
¼ teaspoon salt	2 tablespoons fresh lemon juice
¼ teaspoon freshly ground pepper	

- Combine first 3 ingredients and set aside.

- Remove and discard broccoli leaves and tough ends of stalks. Cut broccoli into spears. Steam broccoli until just crisp-tender, 5 to 8 minutes.

- Arrange on a platter or in a casserole dish. Sprinkle with lemon peel mixture and lemon juice. May be served warm or room temperature, but not chilled.

Serves: 6

Great for people who need to restrict salt... you won't miss it!

Broccoli Casserole

Preparation Time: 15 minutes ~ Cook Time: 30 minutes

1	10-ounce package frozen chopped broccoli	½	cup mayonnaise
2	eggs	1	small or medium onion, chopped
1	10¾-ounce can mushroom soup, undiluted	½	stick butter or margarine, cut in slices
1	cup mild to medium Cheddar cheese, grated		Ritz cracker crumbs

- Cook broccoli according to directions on package. Coat an 8 x 8-inch baking dish with cooking spray.
- Beat 2 eggs and add mushroom soup, cheese, mayonnaise, onion, and butter slices.
- Drain cooked broccoli well and add to the soup mixture. Mix well.
- Pour into baking dish and top with cracker crumbs. Bake at 325 degrees for 30 minutes.

Serves: 8

You can put this together in the morning without the crumbs and cook later in the day, adding crumbs just before baking.

Sunshine Carrots

Preparation Time: 15 minutes ~ Cook Time: 10 to 15 minutes

7-8	carrots, cut into bite-sized pieces	¼	teaspoon ginger
1	tablespoon sugar	¼	cup orange juice
1	teaspoon cornstarch	2	tablespoons butter or margarine
¼	teaspoon salt		Parsley for garnish

- Cook carrots in salted boiling water, 8 to 10 minutes. Drain.
- Meanwhile, combine sugar, cornstarch, salt, and ginger in a small saucepan. Add orange juice. Cook, stirring until mixture bubbles and thickens. Boil 1 minute.
- Stir in butter or margarine. Pour over carrots. Garnish with parsley.

Serves: 6

Carrot and Flake Bake

Preparation Time: 30 minutes ~ Cook Time: 45 to 55 minutes

Carrots

1-1½ pounds carrots, peeled, sliced, cooked, and drained	Dash ground nutmeg
	Dash ground cinnamon
3 eggs	¼ cup butter or margarine, melted
2 tablespoons all-purpose flour	1 teaspoon vanilla extract
1 teaspoon baking powder	

Topping

¼ cup cornflake crumbs	1 tablespoon butter, softened
3 tablespoons light brown sugar	¼ cup walnuts or pecans, chopped, optional

- Puree cooked carrots in blender, food processor, or mixer. Add eggs, one at a time, to carrots and blend well.

- Combine flour, baking powder, nutmeg, and cinnamon. Add to carrots in blender. Add butter and vanilla and puree until smooth.

- Pour into a greased 1½-quart soufflé dish or round baking dish.

- For topping, combine cornflake crumbs, brown sugar, butter, and nuts. Mix well. Sprinkle on top of carrot mixture.

- Bake at 350 degrees, covered with foil, for 20 to 30 minutes. Remove foil and continue baking for another 25 minutes.

Serves: 6 to 8

This carrot dish is my family's favorite vegetable recipe. Every time I make this, it is completely eaten with no leftovers. We tease my red-headed son that he got his red hair from eating so much of this!

Creamed Summer Corn

Preparation Time: 15 minutes ~ Cook Time: 15 minutes

---

4   ears of fresh Silver Queen corn or Super
      Sweet corn
2-3 tablespoons butter

1   tablespoon cornstarch
¾   cup half-and-half
      Salt and pepper, to taste

- Shuck corn and remove all silk. Cut kernels from each ear, "milking" each ear as you go. (This means to run your knife down the length of the ear to push out what remains after you cut the tops of the kernels off.)

- Put corn and butter in a non-stick skillet and cook until the butter is melted. Stir often.

- Mix cornstarch in the cream and pour into the corn and butter mixture. Cook over medium heat, stirring frequently, for about 15 minutes. Add salt and pepper to taste.

Serves: 4 to 6

To reduce fat, replace half-and-half with ¾ cup milk and use only ½ tablespoon cornstarch dissolved in it.

Green Bean Bundles

Preparation Time: 30 minutes ~ Cook Time: 30 minutes

---

1   12-ounce package center-cut bacon,
      40% fat-free
2-3 14.5-ounce cans whole green beans
      Cayenne pepper

1   stick butter or margarine
2   tablespoons garlic powder
1   tablespoon light brown sugar

- Place 15 to 18 green beans on top of a bacon slice and tie up like a package. Continue with remaining beans.

- Sprinkle cayenne over beans. Place all bundles in a 9 x 13-inch baking dish.

- Melt butter and add garlic powder and brown sugar. Blend well. Pour over green beans and bake at 350 degrees for 30 minutes.

Serves: 6

Cran-Apple Crisp

Preparation Time: 20 minutes ~ Cook Time: 45 minutes

Filling

3	cups Rome apples, peeled and cut into squares	2	tablespoons flour
2	cups fresh cranberries	1	cup sugar

Topping

3	packages cinnamon and spice instant oatmeal	½	cup plain flour
¾	cup pecans, chopped	½	cup light brown sugar
		½	cup butter, melted

- Combine 4 filling ingredients together and place in a 9 x 13-inch baking dish.
- Stir all of the topping ingredients together and pour over fruit mixture.
- Bake at 350 degrees, uncovered, for 45 minutes.

Serves: 6 to 8

Great with turkey or ham!

Wonderful Sautéed Mushrooms

Preparation Time: 10 minutes ~ Cook Time: 30 to 35 minutes

2	green onions with tops, chopped	¼	teaspoon salt
¼	cup butter or margarine, melted	¼	teaspoon pepper
1	pound fresh mushrooms, sliced	⅛	teaspoon garlic powder
¼	cup dry white wine	2	teaspoons Worcestershire sauce

- Sauté green onions in butter until tender. Stir in remaining ingredients and cook, uncovered, over low heat for 25 to 30 minutes, or until mushrooms are tender.

Serves: 4

Green Beans with Warm Mustard Vinaigrette

Preparation Time: 15 to 20 minutes
Cook Time: 10 minutes

2   pounds fresh green beans, as thin as possible, ends trimmed
2   shallots, minced
2   tablespoons Dijon mustard
½   cup olive oil
2   tablespoons balsamic vinegar
     Salt and pepper, to taste
¼   cup fresh dill, chopped

- Cook green beans until crisp-tender.

- While beans are still cooking, place shallots, mustard, oil, vinegar, salt, and pepper in small saucepan, whisking constantly over medium heat until mixture is hot.

- Toss the hot beans with the dressing to coat. Quickly add dill, toss to combine, and serve at once.

Serves: 4 to 6

Dressed-Up Green Beans

Preparation Time: 15 minutes
Cook Time: 35 minutes

1   14.5-ounce can French-style green beans, drained
1   15.5-ounce can white shoe-peg corn, drained
1   10.75-ounce can cream of mushroom soup
1   cup sharp Cheddar cheese, grated
½   cup sour cream, may use reduced-fat, not fat-free
1   2.8-ounce can French-fried onions, divided use
1   tube Ritz crackers, crushed
1   stick butter, melted

- Mix together green beans, corn, soup, cheese, sour cream, and half the can of onions. Put in a greased baking dish.

- Mix crushed crackers with butter and spread on top of the vegetable mixture. Bake at 350 degrees for 30 minutes.

- Sprinkle remaining onions on top and bake an additional 5 minutes.

Serves: 6

French-Style Peas

Preparation Time: 5 to 10 minutes ~ Cook Time: 30 minutes

3	tablespoons butter
1	cup lettuce, shredded
½	cup scallions
2	pounds green peas, shelled, or 2 frozen packages, thawed
¾	teaspoon salt
1	teaspoon sugar
2	tablespoons water

- Melt the butter in a deep skillet and spread the lettuce on the bottom. Add the scallions, peas, sugar, salt, and water. Cover and cook over low heat 30 minutes.

- Watch carefully and add a little boiling water if necessary. Mix lightly before serving.

Serves: 4 to 6

Good-As-Gold Potatoes

Preparation Time: 30 minutes
Cook Time: 25 to 20 minutes

8	medium Yukon gold potatoes
½	cup butter or margarine
2	teaspoons salt
¼	teaspoon white pepper
⅔	cup warm milk
1½	cups Cheddar cheese, grated
1	cup heavy cream, whipped to soft peaks

- Peel and boil potatoes until tender. Drain.

- Beat potatoes in a large bowl with electric mixer until fluffy, adding butter, seasonings, and milk. Check seasonings. Spread into a 9 x 13-inch casserole.

- Fold cheese into whipped cream and spread over potatoes for topping. Bake at 350 degrees for 25 to 30 minutes, only until golden brown.

Serves: 8 to 10

Can be made ahead and topping added just before baking.

"The Library" Escalloped Potatoes

Preparation Time: 15 minutes ~ Cook Time: 1 hour and 45 minutes

10 medium Yukon gold potatoes
2½ pints heavy cream

1¼ pounds Gruyère cheese, grated
Salt and pepper, to taste

- Slice potatoes ¼-inch thick and layer in a 3-quart casserole.

- In a saucepan, bring cream to a simmer. Sprinkle Gruyère into cream a little at a time until all cheese is melted. Pour over potatoes. Salt and pepper liberally.

- Bake, covered, 1 hour and 15 minutes at 375 degrees. Remove foil and bake 10 to 15 minutes more until a toothpick inserted in the center is clean. Broil, if necessary, to brown lightly.

Serves: 6 to 8

Garlic Mashed Potatoes

Preparation Time: 20 minutes
Cook Time: 20 minutes

2½ pounds Yukon gold potatoes, peeled and
    cut into ½ inch pieces
3-4 cloves garlic, peeled and quartered

½ cup half-and-half
    (milk may be used, but is not as rich)
5 tablespoons butter, cut into 5 pieces
¼ cup sour cream

- Cook potatoes and garlic in a large pot of boiling, salted water until tender, about 20 minutes. Drain.

- Press potatoes and garlic through a ricer back into the same pot or return potatoes and garlic to pot and use a potato masher to mash.

- Meanwhile, bring half-and-half, butter, and sour cream to a simmer in a small saucepan, or heat in microwave until warm. Do not boil.

- Using an electric beater, whip in the butter, half-and-half, and sour cream until smooth.

Serves: 4 to 6

Hash Brown Potato Casserole

Preparation Time: 10 minutes
Cook Time: 45 to 50 minutes

1	cup sour cream	2	teaspoons salt
1	10.75-ounce can cream of chicken soup	½	cup onion, chopped
1	stick + ¼ cup butter or margarine, melted, divided use	8	ounces sharp Cheddar cheese, grated
1	32-ounce bag frozen hash brown potatoes	2	cups cornflakes, crushed

- Combine the sour cream, soup, and 1 stick butter, then add the potatoes, salt, onion, and cheese. Blend well. Spoon into a greased 9 x 13-inch dish. May freeze at this point.

- When ready to bake, make a topping by combining crushed cornflakes with ¼ cup melted butter or margarine. Sprinkle over top of casserole. Bake at 350 degrees for 45 to 50 minutes.

Serves: 8 to 10

Add a pinch of baking soda for fluffier mashed potatoes.

Creamy Potato Puff

Preparation Time: 30 minutes
Cook Time: 1 hour plus 50 minutes

4	large baking potatoes, 10 ounces each	1	teaspoon salt
8	ounces cream cheese, softened	¼	teaspoon pepper
1	medium onion, finely chopped	1	3-ounce can French fried onion rings
3	eggs	4	tablespoons dry sherry, optional
3	tablespoons flour		

- Bake potatoes until done. Scoop out insides and mash in a large bowl. Add cream cheese and beat until smooth. Add onion, eggs, flour, salt, and pepper. Beat until light and fluffy.

- Spoon into a greased round 3-quart soufflé dish. Sprinkle onion rings on top. Drizzle with sherry, if desired.

- Cover with foil and bake at 325 degrees for 30 minutes, then remove foil and continue cooking for 20 minutes.

Serves: 6 to 8

May be refrigerated up to 2 days. May also be frozen.

Red Beans and Rice

Preparation Time: 15 minutes
Cook Time: 1 hour and 30 minutes to 2 hours

1   28-ounce can diced tomatoes with juice
1   8-ounce can tomato sauce
1   16-ounce can chicken broth
1   bay leaf
2   tablespoons Worcestershire sauce
1   teaspoon Tabasco sauce
½   teaspoon pepper
1   teaspoon oregano

1   teaspoon cumin
1   40-ounce can plus 1 (16-ounce) can kidney beans, rinsed and drained
3   cloves garlic, minced
2   onions, chopped
16 ounces kielbasa, sliced
    Salt and pepper, to taste
    Cooked white rice

•   In a 5-quart Dutch oven, bring first 9 ingredients to a slow boil. Add beans, garlic, onion, and kielbasa. Bring back to a boil. Season with salt and pepper.

•   Cover and bake at 350 degrees 1 to 1½ hours. Can also be simmered on stovetop. Serve with white rice.

Serves: 8

Mushroom Rice

Preparation Time: 30 minutes   ~   Cook Time: 1 hour

2½-3 pounds fresh mushrooms, sliced
      (any variety)
      Olive oil
1   onion, chopped

2   cups uncooked rice, basmati is best
2   10.75-ounce cans beef broth
2   10.75-ounce cans beef consommé

•   Sauté mushrooms in a couple of tablespoons of olive oil. Sauté onion in olive oil.

•   Combine mushrooms and onion in a 9 x 13-inch baking dish. Add uncooked rice, broth, and consommé (dish will be very liquidy).

•   Cook 1 hour at 350 degrees.

Serves: 10 to 12

This recipe can be halved and is very good with grilled beef, chicken, or fish.

Spicy Creamed Spinach

Preparation Time: 15 minutes
Cook Time: 15 minutes

2	10-ounce packages frozen chopped spinach	¾	teaspoon celery salt
4	tablespoons butter	¾	teaspoon garlic salt
2	tablespoons flour		Salt, to taste
2	tablespoons onion, chopped	1	teaspoon Worcestershire sauce
½	cup evaporated milk		Cayenne, to taste
½	cup vegetable liquid	6	ounces Monterey Jack cheese with jalapeños, grated
½	teaspoon black pepper		

- Cook spinach according to directions on box. Drain well and reserve liquid.

- Melt butter in saucepan over low heat. Add flour, stirring until blended and smooth, but not brown.

- Add onion and cook until soft, but not brown. Add liquid slowly, whisking constantly to avoid lumps. Cook until smooth and thick.

- Add seasonings and cheese. Stir until melted.

- Combine with cooked spinach. May be served immediately or put into a casserole and topped with buttered bread or cracker crumbs.

Serves: 6 to 8

Spinach and Artichokes

Preparation Time: 25 minutes ~ Cook Time: 30 minutes

3	10-ounce packages frozen spinach, cooked and drained well
2	15-ounce cans artichoke bottoms, diced finely
10	ounces cream cheese, softened
1	tablespoon butter
½	cup onions, chopped and sautéed
1	teaspoon salt
½	teaspoon pepper
1	cup Swiss cheese, grated
	Parmesan cheese, grated

- Combine spinach, artichoke bottoms, cream cheese, butter, onion, salt, and pepper.

- Place in a 9 x 13-inch baking dish and top with Swiss cheese. Bake at 350 degrees for 30 minutes, or until bubbly. Sprinkle Parmesan cheese over the top before serving.

Serves: 8 to 10

Spinach Gratin

Preparation Time: 30 minutes ~ Cook Time: 40 to 45 minutes

1	pound fresh spinach, washed with stems removed or 1 package frozen spinach
1	large onion, chopped
1	clove garlic, minced or pressed
3	tablespoons unsalted butter
4	eggs plus 2 egg whites
6	ounces cream cheese
½	cup Muenster or mild cheese, grated
¼	cup plus 2 to 3 tablespoons grated Parmesan cheese, divided use
	Fresh ground pepper and nutmeg

- Sauté spinach with onion and garlic in butter over medium heat until most of the moisture has evaporated. Drain and reserve.

- Beat eggs several minutes in processor or mixer with cheeses, pepper, and nutmeg. Add spinach and blend well.

- Butter or spray a 9-inch quiche dish and pour spinach into dish. Sprinkle with 2 to 3 table-spoons Parmesan. Bake at 375 degrees for 40 to 45 minutes.

Serves: 8 to 10 as a side dish, 4 to 6 as an entrée

Spinach Stuffed
Vidalia Onions

Preparation Time: 30 minutes ~ Cook Time: 15 to 20 minutes

4	medium Vidalia onions	Salt and pepper, to taste
1	pound fresh spinach	Dash cayenne pepper
2	tablespoons unsalted butter, melted	2-3 tablespoons Parmesan cheese, grated
¼	cup light cream	

- Peel and core onions. Place in a steamer basket over simmering (not boiling) water and steam until onions are softened but still firm in shape, approximately 5 to 10 minutes. Remove from heat and cool.

- Wash spinach thoroughly and remove stems. Cook 1 minute in the water remaining on the leaves after the washing. Drain and chop.

- Sauté spinach after chopping in melted butter. Add the cream and cook until fairly dry over medium heat. Season with salt and pepper.

- Fill the cooled onions with spinach mixture. Sprinkle with cayenne pepper and cheese.

- Bake at 350 degrees in a shallow pan greased with cooking spray until heated throughout.

Serves: 4

You can also wrap each onion individually in aluminum foil and place on the grill to heat while steaks, chops, or chicken cook.

Cranberry Pecan Stuffing

Preparation Time: 20 minutes ~ Cook Time: 30 to 45 minutes

¼ cup + 3 tablespoons butter or margarine, divided use
2 stalks celery, chopped
1 large onion, chopped

1 14½-ounce can chicken broth
1 16-ounce package herb-seasoned stuffing
½ cup cranberries
½ cup pecans, chopped

- In a 4-quart saucepan over medium heat, melt ¼ cup butter and cook celery and onion until tender. Add broth and heat to boiling.

- Remove from heat. Add stuffing, cranberries, and nuts; toss to mix well.

- Stuff bird cavity with mixture or bake stuffing in a buttered 9 x 13-inch pan and dot with 3 tablespoons butter.

- Bake at 350 degrees for 30 to 45 minutes until lightly browned.

Serves: 6

Sweet Potato Casserole

Preparation Time: 30 minutes ~ Cook Time: 30 to 40 minutes

3 cups sweet potatoes, mashed, may use canned or fresh, baked
⅓ cup granulated sugar
3 eggs
½ cup milk

1 tablespoon vanilla
½ stick butter, divided use
½ cup flour
⅔ cup light brown sugar
½ cup pecan pieces

- Combine sweet potatoes, granulated sugar, eggs, milk, vanilla, and ¼ stick butter. Put into buttered 1½ to 2-quart casserole.

- In a bowl, mash together remaining ¼ stick butter, flour, and brown sugar with a fork to make topping. Sprinkle on top of casserole, then add pecans to the top.

- Bake, uncovered, at 350 degrees for 30 to 40 minutes.

Serves: 6

Southern Cornbread Stuffing

Preparation Time: 1 hour
Cook Time: 30 to 35 minutes, when cooking separately from bird.

Cornbread

2	eggs	1	teaspoon baking powder
3	tablespoons salad oil	½	teaspoon baking soda
1	cup plain yogurt or buttermilk	1½	cups yellow cornmeal
1	teaspoon salt	½	cup flour
1	teaspoon sugar		

Stuffing

1	pound bulk sausage, hot or mild, sage-seasoned is best	1	teaspoon poultry seasoning or dried sage (or 1 tablespoon fresh sage, minced)
1	cup onion, finely chopped	1	teaspoon salt
1	cup celery, finely chopped	½	cup pecans, chopped

- Beat the eggs lightly. Add the oil and yogurt and whisk together.

- In a separate bowl, combine the salt, sugar, baking powder, baking soda, cornmeal, and flour.

- Combine cornmeal mixture with egg mixture until just blended. Bake in a buttered 9 x 13-inch pan at 400 degrees for 25 minutes or until nicely browned. (Makes 6 cups of cornbread for the stuffing.)

- While cornbread is cooking, brown the sausage in a large skillet over medium heat. Break it up with a fork into small pieces as it cooks. Remove the sausage with a slotted spoon.

- Sauté the onion and celery in the sausage drippings until soft, but not browned.

- Break the cornbread into very small pieces in a large bowl. Add the poultry seasoning, salt, sausage, onions, celery, and pecans. Blend well and use to stuff a turkey or large roasting hen. This is enough stuffing for an 18 to 20-pound turkey.

- If baking separately, bake in a buttered lasagna pan and dot with butter. Bake at 350 degrees for 30 to 35 minutes or until browned.

Serves: 10 to 12

Rice-Filled Tomatoes

Preparation Time: 30 minutes
Cook Time: 45 minutes

4	ripe beefsteak tomatoes	1	celery stalk, finely chopped
	Salt and freshly ground pepper, to taste	2	tablespoons fresh basil, chopped, divided use
5	ounces cooked rice		
1	tablespoon pine nuts	2	teaspoons balsamic vinegar
1	tablespoon raisins, soaked in hot water	2	tablespoons olive oil

- Slice a lid off the tomatoes, reserve. Scoop out flesh and sprinkle inside of tomatoes with salt. Invert and drain on paper towels for 15 minutes.

- Sieve tomato pulp and add seeded mixture into the cooked rice with pine nuts, raisins, celery, and half the basil. Season to taste with salt and pepper.

- Fill the tomatoes with the rice mixture. Replace tomato lids. Place the tomatoes in an oiled shallow casserole dish and bake in the oven at 325 degrees for 45 minutes.

- Whisk the vinegar with the oil. Remove the tomatoes from the oven, take off the lids and drizzle each one with the oil and vinegar. Replace the lids and leave to cool.

- Serve at room temperature, using remaining basil for garnish.

Serves: 4

Desserts

Amaretto and Almond Cheesecake

Preparation Time: 30 minutes
Cook Time: 60 minutes
Prepare ahead.

Crust
50 vanilla wafers (¾ of a box)
½ cup granulated sugar

½ cup almonds, chopped
½ cup butter, melted

Filling
24 ounces cream cheese, softened
⅔ cup granulated sugar
1 cup sour cream
4 eggs, beaten

½ cup Amaretto liquor
Kiwi or strawberries
(dipped in chocolate perhaps!)

- For crust, grind wafers, sugar, and almonds in food processor. Add melted butter and stir just until blended. Press crust mixture into bottom and up sides of a 9-inch springform pan.

- For filling, beat cream cheese and sugar until smooth. Blend in sour cream, eggs, and Amaretto.

- Pour into prepared pan, and bake for 1 hour in an oven preheated to 350 degrees. Turn oven off after 1 hour and crack door. Leave cheesecake in oven for 1 more hour.

- Remove and chill overnight in refrigerator. Garnish before serving. Best prepared a day ahead.

Serves: 8

Mocha Cheesecake

Preparation Time: 20 minutes
Cook Time: 50 to 60 minutes
Prepare ahead.

Cake

1	cup chocolate chip cookie crumbs, or shortbread cookies sprinkled with ground chocolate chips
2	tablespoons butter
½	cup strong coffee
1¼	cups semisweet chocolate, melted

24	ounces cream cheese
½	cup granulated sugar
½	cup brown sugar
1	cup sour cream
3	eggs, at room temperature
1	tablespoon vanilla extract

Glaze

¾ cup semi-sweet chocolate, coarsely chopped   ¼ cup butter

- For cake, grind cookie crumbs and butter. Press into a buttered springform pan. Chill crust while preparing filling.

- Combine warm (not too hot) coffee and melted chocolate. Set aside.

- In a separate bowl, beat cream cheese until smooth. Add sugar, brown sugar, and sour cream. Continue beating, adding eggs. Add the coffee/chocolate mixture and vanilla.

- Pour into prepared crust. Bake 50 to 60 minutes at 350 degrees. Turn oven off, and crack the door. Leave cheesecake in the oven for 1 more hour. Remove and cool.

- For glaze, melt semi-sweet chocolate with butter. Pour over cooled cake. Chill 3 to 4 hours before serving.

Serves: 8 to 10

The Great
Pumpkin Cheesecake

Preparation Time: 20 minutes
Cook Time: 1 hour and 30 to 45 minutes
Prepare ahead.

2 tablespoons butter, softened	1 teaspoon ground allspice
⅓ cup gingersnap crumbs	½ teaspoon ground ginger
32 ounces cream cheese	¼ teaspoon salt
1½ cups brown sugar, firmly packed	2 cups pumpkin puree
5 eggs, at room temperature	Maple syrup
¼ cup all-purpose flour	Walnut halves or pecans, toasted
1 teaspoon ground cinnamon	

- Generously butter a 9-inch springform pan with softened butter. Sprinkle gingersnap crumbs to coat bottom and sides evenly.

- Beat cream cheese until fluffy. Gradually add brown sugar. Add eggs, 1 at a time, beating well after each addition. Sift in flour, cinnamon, allspice, ginger, and salt. Blend well. Beat in pumpkin puree.

- Pour into prepared pan. Bake at 325 degrees in center of oven 1½ to 1¾ hours, until cake pulls away from sides of pan and toothpick comes out clean.

- Remove from oven, cool for 1 hour. Carefully remove from pan and continue cooling. Refrigerate. Brush top with syrup and sprinkle with nuts.

Serves: 8 to 10

Angel Sherry Cake

Preparation Time: 45 minutes
Prepare ahead.

1 envelope of gelatin	½ cup plus 1 tablespoon sherry, divided use
½ cup cold milk	1 pint whipping cream
4 eggs	1 large angel food cake
1 cup granulated sugar, divided use	1 cup almond slivers, toasted

- Soak gelatin in milk.

- Separate 4 eggs. Beat yolks with ½ cup sugar and ½ cup sherry. Cook in double boiler until mixture coats spoon. Stir in gelatin while still hot and pour into large bowl.

- Beat egg whites until stiff, adding ¼ cup sugar, slowly. Fold egg white mixture into custard mixture.

- Beat whipping cream until soft peaks form. Slowly add remaining ¼ cup sugar. Reserve about ⅓ of the cream mixture, and fold the rest into custard mixture.

- Rinse large cake mold with cold water. Shake off excess water, but do not dry. Break up the angel food cake into bite-sized pieces. Sprinkle a layer of cake on bottom of pan. Follow with a layer of custard. Alternate layering until cake and custard are gone. Cover and refrigerate overnight.

- Unmold onto cake plate. Ice with reserved whipping cream seasoned with 1 tablespoon sherry. Sprinkle toasted almonds over cake.

Serves: 8 to 10

 Egg whites yield more volume if beaten at room temperature with a pinch of cream of tartar and if they are beaten in a copper bowl.

Fresh Berry Trifle

Preparation Time: 20 minutes plus 3 hours refrigeration time
Prepare ahead.

2	pints strawberries	1½	teaspoons vanilla extract
2	pints blueberries	3	cups chilled whipping cream
2	pints raspberries	48	lady fingers
¼	cup granulated sugar	1	cup raspberry jam, seedless

- Mix berries, sugar, and vanilla in a large bowl. Let stand 5 minutes.

- Beat chilled cream in a separate bowl until peaks form.

- Arrange lady fingers in large glass bowl to cover bottom. Spread ⅓ of the jam on ladyfingers, top with fruit mixture, then the whipped cream. Repeat layers.

- Refrigerate trifle 3 hours or more before serving.

Serves: 6 to 8

Whipping cream will yield more volume if the cream and the bowl in which it is to be whipped are placed in the freezer for 5 minutes before whipping.

Chocolate Pound Cake

Preparation Time: 30 minutes ~ Cook Time: 1 hour and 15 minutes
Prepare ahead.

Cake

3	cups cake flour
4	tablespoons cocoa powder
½	teaspoon salt
1	teaspoon baking powder
1	cup butter, at room temperature

½	cup solid vegetable shortening
3	cups granulated sugar
5	eggs, at room temperature
1	tablespoon vanilla extract
1	cup milk

Frosting

4	cups powdered sugar
4	tablespoons cocoa powder
½	cup butter

1	teaspoon vanilla extract
	Milk, just a bit!

- For cake, butter and flour Bundt or tube pan.

- Sift flour, cocoa, salt, and baking powder. Cream butter and shortening with an electric mixer, gradually adding sugar. Add eggs, one at a time, then add vanilla.

- Add sifted ingredients and milk alternately and mix well. Bake at 325 degrees for 1 hour and 15 minutes. Cool.

- For frosting, mix powdered sugar and cocoa powder. Melt butter and add to sugar mixture. Add vanilla. Add milk until spreading consistency is reached. Spread over cooled cake.

Serves: 8 to 10

"Heart-Pounding" Cake

Preparation Time: 45 minutes
Cook Time: 1 hour and 30 minutes

½ teaspoon baking soda	3 cups all-purpose flour
1 cup sour cream	1 teaspoon vanilla extract
1 cup butter, at room temperature	1 teaspoon orange extract
3 cups granulated sugar	1 teaspoon lemon extract
6 eggs, at room temperature	

- Combine baking soda and sour cream, let rest 30 minutes. Butter and flour tube or Bundt pan.

- Cream together butter and sugar. Add eggs, one at a time, beating well after each addition.

- Alternately add flour and sour cream mixture, beginning and ending with flour. Add extracts. Pour into prepared pan. Bake at 300 degrees for 1½ hours.

Serves: 10 to 12

My mother would make this pound cake for the family every Saturday. When the cake was done, she would cut a slice, pour a glass of cold milk, and then call me to the kitchen. This is my very favorite cake to this day and it still goes great with milk!

Headmaster's Sunday Best Cake

Preparation Time: 30 minutes
Cook Time: 25 minutes

Cake

½	cup butter
½	cup solid vegetable shortening
2	cups granulated sugar
5	egg yolks, at room temperature
2	cups all-purpose flour, sifted
1	teaspoon baking soda

1	cup buttermilk
1	teaspoon vanilla extract
1	cup coconut
1	cup pecans, chopped
5	egg whites, at room temperature stiffly beaten

Frosting

8	ounces cream cheese, softened
¼	cup butter, softened
4	cups powdered sugar, sifted

1	teaspoon vanilla extract
½	cup pecans, chopped

- For cake, cream together butter and shortening. Add sugar and beat until smooth. Add egg yolks and beat well.

- Combine flour and soda, and add to creamed mixture alternately with buttermilk. Stir in vanilla, coconut, and nuts. Fold in stiffly beaten egg whites.

- Bake at 350 degrees in 3 buttered and floured 8-inch cake pans for 25 minutes or until done. Cool in the pans for 10 minutes before removing to racks.

- For frosting, beat cream cheese and butter until smooth. Add powdered sugar and mix well. Add vanilla and beat until smooth. Stir in the nuts. Ice cake with cream cheese frosting after completely cool.

Serves: 10 to 12

Heavenly
White Chocolate Cake

Preparation Time: 20 minutes ~ Cook Time: 30 minutes
Prepare ahead.

Cake

¾	cup white chocolate
4	eggs, separated and at room temperature
1	cup butter, room temperature
2	cups granulated sugar

1	teaspoon vanilla extract
2½	cups all-purpose flour
1	teaspoon baking powder
1	cup buttermilk

Frosting

1½	cups granulated sugar
2	egg whites
¼	teaspoon salt

⅓	cup water
¼	teaspoon cream of tartar
1	teaspoon vanilla

- For cake, butter and flour 3 (9-inch) cake pans.

- Melt chocolate in double boiler or microwave, stir until smooth, and cool to room temperature. Beat 4 egg whites until stiff and place in refrigerator until needed.

- Cream butter and sugar until smooth and light, 8 to 10 minutes. Beat in 4 yolks, one at a time. Add vanilla and melted chocolate.

- Combine flour and baking powder. Add to butter mixture alternately with buttermilk, beginning and ending with flour. Fold in egg whites.

- Pour batter into cake pans and bake at 350 degrees for about 30 minutes. Cake is done when toothpick comes out clean. Cool in pan about 5 minutes, then turn out onto racks to finish cooling.

- For frosting, combine sugar, egg whites, salt, water, and cream of tartar in top of double boiler. Beat well. Place over pan of rapidly boiling water and beat constantly 7 minutes or until icing holds a peak. Remove from heat and add vanilla. Beat until cool and thick enough to spread.

- Spread icing between layers. Ice top and sides.

Serves: 8 to 12

Option: For Heavenly Coconut White Chocolate Cake, add 1 teaspoon coconut extract to batter when adding the vanilla. Sprinkle 3 cups freshly grated or canned coconut between the layers, on the top and on the sides of cake.

Fresh Apple Cake

Preparation Time: 30 to 40 minutes ~ Cook Time: 1 hour
Prepare ahead.

Cake

2	cups granulated sugar	1	teaspoon ground cinnamon
1	cup vegetable oil	1	teaspoon ground nutmeg
3	eggs, at room temperature	1	teaspoon salt
2½	cups all-purpose flour	2	teaspoons vanilla extract
1	teaspoon baking soda	4	cups apples, peeled and diced
2	teaspoons baking powder	1	cup pecans or walnuts, chopped

Brown Butter Glaze

½	cup brown sugar, firmly packed	¼	cup evaporated milk
½	cup butter	1	teaspoon vanilla extract

- For cake, butter and flour Bundt pan. Cream sugar and oil well. Beat in eggs one at a time.

- Sift together flour, baking soda, baking powder, cinnamon, nutmeg, and salt and blend into creamed mixture. Add vanilla. Fold in apples and pecans.

- Pour into prepared pan. Bake at 350 degrees for 1 hour or until done. Cool.

- For glaze, combine brown sugar, butter, and milk in a medium saucepan. Bring to a full boil and cook, stirring constantly for 2 minutes. Remove from heat and stir in vanilla. Beat until glaze is cool.

- When cake and glaze are cool, spoon on glaze-it is runny, but keep on spooning!

Serves: 8 to 12

Nectar of the Gods Cake

Preparation Time: 20 minutes
Cook Time: 1 hour

Cake
1   box Lemon Supreme cake mix
½   cup vegetable oil
5   ounces apricot nectar
½   cup granulated sugar

4   eggs, at room temperature
1   teaspoon lemon extract
     Rind of 1 lemon, grated

Glaze
¾   cup powdered sugar
     Juice of 1 lemon or ¼ cup apricot nectar

1   teaspoon Cointreau

- For cake, butter and flour tube pan.

- Place all ingredients in mixing bowl. Beat for 8 to 10 minutes. Pour into prepared pan. Bake at 325 degrees for 1 hour. Cool in pan for 5 minutes, turn on to rack.

- For glaze, mix glaze ingredients while cake is baking. Stir until it is of a drizzling consistency. Glaze while cake is still warm.

Serves: 8 to 12

Dust cake with flour or cornstarch before icing so the icing won't run off.

Peter Rabbit's
Favorite Carrot Cake

Preparation Time: 20 minutes ~ Cook Time: 20 to 25 minutes
Prepare ahead.

Cake

4	eggs, at room temperature
2	cups granulated sugar
1½	cups vegetable oil
2	cups all-purpose flour
2	teaspoons ground cinnamon
2	teaspoons baking soda

2	teaspoons baking powder
1	teaspoon salt
3	cups carrots, grated
1	cup raisins, macerated in orange juice, drained

Frosting

8	ounces cream cheese, softened
½	cup butter, softened
4	cups powdered sugar

1	teaspoon vanilla
2	tablespoons orange juice concentrate
1½	cups nuts, toasted and chopped

- For cake, butter and flour 3 (8-inch) cake pans.

- In a large bowl, beat eggs until frothy. Add sugar gradually. Beat until light and lemon colored. Slowly add oil, beating until combined.

- In a separate bowl, sift together flour, cinnamon, baking soda, baking powder, and salt. Fold dry ingredients by thirds into egg mixture. Add carrots and raisins, mixing well.

- Pour batter into prepared pans. Bake at 325 degrees for 20 to 25 minutes or until toothpick comes out clean. Cool before frosting.

- For frosting, cream together cream cheese and butter. Whip in sugar, vanilla, and orange juice. Stir in nuts. Frost cake.

Serves: 8

Torta di Cioccolato

Preparation Time: 20 minutes ~ Cook Time: 50 to 55 minutes
Prepare ahead.

2	cups butter	12	ounces bittersweet chocolate
1	cup granulated sugar	4	ounces semi-sweet chocolate
1	cup brewed coffee	9	eggs, at room temperature, lightly beaten

- Preheat oven to 350 degrees. Butter and flour a 9-inch springform pan.

- In a large saucepan, over low heat, melt butter, sugar, and coffee. Add chocolate and continue to stir until melted. Remove from heat.

- Add eggs and whisk until thoroughly incorporated into chocolate mixture. Pour into a 9-inch springform pan.

- Bake at 350 degrees for 50 to 55 minutes. Cake is done when top has a thin crust and is dry to the touch.

- Refrigerate up to 24 hours before serving.

Serves: 8 to 10

Use cocoa rather than flour to dust pans for chocolate cake.

Simply the Best
Chocolate Cake

Preparation Time: 1 hour ~ Cook Time: 29 to 35 minutes

2	large eggs, at room temperature	½	cup sour cream
1⅓	cups sugar	1½	teaspoons vanilla
2	ounces unsweetened chocolate, chopped into small pieces	1½	cups cake flour
		½	cup unsweetened Dutch-style cocoa
¾	cup lightly salted butter, cut into 8 to 10 pieces	1	teaspoon baking soda
		1	cup milk, warmed to tepid

- Place oven rack in center of oven heated to 350 degrees. Butter and flour 2 (8-inch) round cake pans. Reserve.

- Beat eggs in a large mixer bowl at high speed 1 minute. Continue beating, adding sugar VERY slowly, about 7 minutes.

- Melt chocolate with butter over a double boiler that has been removed from the heat source. Beating at low speed, drizzle the warm chocolate into the egg mixture. Add sour cream and vanilla, beating at low speed until thoroughly blended.

- Sift together flour, cocoa, and baking soda. While beating at low speed, add dry ingredients, about ½ cup at a time, to chocolate mixture alternating with milk, about ⅓ cup at a time. Stop beating mixture, as necessary, to scrape the sides of the bowl with a spatula. Beat until well blended.

- Divide the batter between the two cake pans. Put both pans diagonally on the same rack. Bake 29 to 35 minutes, or until a toothpick inserted into the cake comes out clean. Cool cakes in pans on wire racks until barely warm. Remove from pans and cool completely on racks.

- Prepare buttercream recipe (see next page). Assemble cake by placing 1 layer on a serving plate. Spread top with about ¾ cup of the buttercream. Refrigerate for 15 minutes. Add the second layer on top of the first layer. Frost sides, then top of the cake. Refrigerate. (Cake must be stored in the refrigerator.)

Serves: 12 to 16

Simply the Best Chocolate Buttercream

5 ounces semisweet chocolate, chopped into pieces
1 ounce bitter chocolate, chopped into pieces
1 cup butter, slightly softened, divided use

1½ tablespoons dark rum or cognac
1 large egg, at room temperature
4 large egg yolks, at room temperature
½ cup sugar
⅓ cup water

- Melt chocolate with 2 tablespoons of the butter in a double boiler that has been removed from the heat source. Add the liquor. Place whole egg and egg yolks in a medium mixing bowl. Beat at high speed 1 minute. Reserve.

- Measure sugar and water into a non-aluminum saucepan. Stir well. Cook over low heat until simmering. Cover and simmer 3 minutes. Uncover and raise heat to medium-high. Boil until syrup reaches the soft ball stage, 234 degrees on a candy thermometer.

- While beating the eggs at high speed, immediately drizzle the syrup into the eggs. Continue beating until the bottom of the bowl is cool to touch. Gradually beat the melted chocolate into the egg mixture until thoroughly blended.

- Place the remaining butter in a small mixing bowl and beat at medium speed until fluffy. While beating the chocolate mixture at high speed, add the butter, about 1 tablespoon at a time. When all the butter has been added, beat about 5 minutes.

- Refrigerate buttercream, stirring twice, for about 30 minutes, until firm enough to spread.

Black Bottom Cupcakes

Preparation Time: 15 minutes ~ Cook Time: 20 to 25 minutes

8	ounces cream cheese	1	teaspoon baking soda
1	egg, at room temperature	¼	cup cocoa powder
1⅓	cups granulated sugar, divided use	1	cup water
⅛	teaspoon plus ½ teaspoon salt, divided use	⅓	cup vegetable oil
6	ounces semi-sweet chocolate morsels	1	tablespoon vinegar
1½	cups all-purpose flour	1	teaspoon vanilla extract

- Cream the cream cheese, egg, ⅓ cup sugar, and ⅛ teaspoon salt until smooth. Add chocolate morsels, set aside.

- In a separate bowl, mix remaining ingredients and fill paper cupcake holders ⅓ to ½ full. Top each with heaping tablespoon of the cream cheese mixture.

- Bake at 350 degrees for 20 to 25 minutes.

Yield: 20 to 25 cupcakes

Tortoni

Preparation Time: 30 minutes ~ Cook Time: 20 minutes
Prepare ahead. Keep frozen.

1	cup all-purpose flour	½	cup maraschino cherries, chopped
½	cup walnuts, finely chopped	4	ounces sweet chocolate, shaved
½	cup brown sugar	1	teaspoon fresh lemon rind, grated
½	cup butter, melted	1	teaspoon fresh orange rind, grated
½	gallon vanilla ice cream, softened	1	cup slivered almonds, lightly toasted

- Mix flour, chopped walnuts, brown sugar, and melted butter. Spread on a cookie sheet. Bake at 350 degrees for 20 minutes stirring occasionally.

- Cool slightly, but do not allow to harden. Form crust into bottom and up sides of a 9-inch springform pan.

- Mix ice cream, cherries, shaved chocolate, lemon zest, orange zest, and almonds. Pour into crust and freeze.

Serves: 8

Chocolate Mousse

**Preparation Time: 10 minutes ~ Refrigerate 1 hour and 30 minutes to 2 hours.
Prepare ahead.**

---

12 ounces semi-sweet chocolate morsels
½ cup boiling water
8 eggs, separated, at room temperature

¼ cup dark rum, cognac, Kahlúa or Frangelico
Pinch cream of tartar
2 cups whipped cream

- Chop chocolate into small pieces or grind in a food processor. With the processor running add the boiling water to the chocolate. Continue processing, adding the egg yolks, one at a time. Then add liqueur. Set aside.

- Beat egg whites until foamy. Add cream of tartar and beat until soft peaks form. Gently fold chocolate into egg whites.

- Pour into dessert glasses. Cover with plastic wrap and refrigerate 1½ to 2 hours. Serve with whipped cream.

Serves: 8

Option: Halve the recipe and pour into pre-baked pie or tart shell, top with whipped cream and chocolate curls.

When melting chocolate with butter, melt the butter first to help prevent chocolate from "seizing" (the cocoa solids separate from the fat).

Chocolate Mocha Soufflé

Preparation Time: 40 minutes
Cook Time: 30 minutes

⅓	cup all-purpose flour	3	tablespoons butter, softened
1	tablespoon instant coffee	6	eggs, separated, at room temperature
1¼	cups granulated sugar	2	teaspoons vanilla extract
1	cup milk, lukewarm	½	teaspoon salt
6	ounces unsweetened chocolate, broken into pieces		

- In a 3-quart saucepan, heat flour, coffee, and sugar. Slowly whisk in milk. Cook over medium heat, stirring constantly, until thickens and boils. Boil 1 minute. Remove from heat.

- Stir chocolate pieces and butter into mixture until smooth. Beat in yolks all at once until well blended. Stir in vanilla. Set aside to cool.

- Grease 6 (8-ounce) soufflé dishes with butter and sprinkle with sugar. In large bowl, beat egg whites and salt until stiff peaks form. Gently fold chocolate into whites.

- Divide evenly among prepared dishes and bake at 350 degrees for 30 minutes. Serve immediately.

Serves: 6

If chocolate "seizes" when melting, add a little vegetable shortening immediately.

Coastal Carolina Wine "Jelly"

Preparation Time: 10 minutes
Chill Time: 6 hours
Prepare ahead.

Jelly
¼	cup cold water
2	packages gelatin
2	cups boiling water
1	cup sugar

⅔	cup orange juice
¼	cup lemon juice
¾	cup cream sherry
⅓	cup bourbon

Topping
½	pint whipping cream
2	tablespoons powdered sugar

1	scant tablespoon Grand Marnier

- For jelly, in a 2-quart glass measuring cup, soften gelatin in cold water for 5 minutes. Add boiling water to gelatin and stir until dissolved. Add sugar and stir until dissolved. Add juices, sherry, and bourbon.

- Divide evenly among 6 dessert glasses. Chill at least 6 hours.

- For topping, whip cream with powdered sugar, to form soft peaks. Add Grand Marnier and whip 10 more seconds. Spoon whipped cream over gelatin.

Serves: 6

A lovely light dessert and after-dinner drink all in one!

Bread Pudding with Lemon Sauce

Preparation Time: 20 minutes ~ Cook Time: 1 hour

Pudding

4	large eggs	1	cup raisins
¾	cup granulated sugar	4	cups dried bread (stale is best), cubed
1	cup evaporated milk	¾	stick butter (6 tablespoons), melted
1½	cups whole milk		Dash nutmeg
2	teaspoons vanilla extract		

Lemon Sauce

1	cup sugar	1	lemon rind, grated
1	cup water	2	tablespoons cornstarch
3	tablespoons lemon juice		

- For pudding, beat eggs lightly in a mixing bowl. Add sugar, then milk, vanilla, and raisins.

- Stir cubed bread into the milk mixture. Pour into a buttered 2-quart casserole dish. Pour melted butter over the top and sprinkle with nutmeg. Bake at 350 degrees for 1 hour.

- For lemon sauce, just before serving, bring sauce ingredients to boil over medium heat and then remove to thicken. Serve over warm pudding.

Serves: 6 to 8

Microwave citrus fruits 30 to 60 seconds on high before juicing to increase the amount of juice extracted.

"Can't Catch Me" Gingerbread

Preparation Time: 10 minutes ~ Cook Time: 25 to 30 minutes

1½ cups all-purpose flour	½ cup butter, room temperature
½ teaspoon baking soda	½ cup sugar
¼ teaspoon salt	1 egg
½ teaspoon ground cinnamon	½ cup molasses
½ teaspoon ground ginger	½ cup buttermilk
½ teaspoon allspice	

- Butter and flour an 11 x 7 x 1½-inch pan. Mix together the flour, baking soda, salt, cinnamon, ginger, and allspice. Set aside.

- Cream butter. Add sugar and egg. Cream until light and fluffy.

- Add molasses. Beat vigorously for 2 minutes. Add flour mixture gradually, alternately with buttermilk. Beat well after each addition.

- Pour batter into a prepared pan and bake at 350 degrees for 25 to 30 minutes.

- Cool for 5 minutes before removing from pan. Serve with lemon curd or fresh whipped cream.

Serves: 12 to 15

Pecos Bill Bars

Preparation Time: 30 minutes ~ Cook Time: 65 minutes

1 box yellow cake mix	1 cup dark corn syrup
⅓ cup vegetable oil	1 cup sugar
5 large eggs, at room temperature, divided use	¼ cup butter, melted
	2 cups pecans, chopped

- Combine cake mix, oil, and 1 egg. Mixture will be crumbly. Press into bottom of buttered 13 x 9-inch pan. Bake at 350 degrees for 20 minutes.

- Beat remaining 4 eggs, corn syrup, sugar, and butter until smooth. Add pecans and pour over bottom layer.

- Bake for 45 minutes or until filling is set. Cool completely before cutting.

Serves: 12 to 16

Crème de Menthe Bars

Preparation Time: 1 hour ~ Cook Time: 15 minutes
Prepare ahead.

---

3 squares unsweetened chocolate	4 cups powdered sugar
⅔ cup vegetable oil	2 tablespoons milk
2 cups brown sugar, packed	1 cup plus 2 tablespoons butter, divided use
3 eggs	3 ounces crème de menthe liqueur
1¼ cups all-purpose flour	½ teaspoon peppermint extract
½ teaspoon salt	Dash green food coloring
½ teaspoon baking soda	6 ounces chocolate chips
1 teaspoon vanilla extract	

- Melt chocolate squares and oil. Mix with brown sugar, eggs, flour , salt, soda, and vanilla.

- Spread into a greased jelly-roll pan. Bake at 350 degrees for 15 minutes. Cool.

- Beat powdered sugar, milk, 1 cup butter, crème de menthe, peppermint extract, and food coloring. Spread over cooled crust and refrigerate until firm.

- Melt chocolate chips with 2 tablespoons butter. When smooth, spread on top of cooled layers. Store in the refrigerator.

Yield: 40 squares

The Perfect Brownie

Preparation Time: 20 minutes ~ Cook Time: 25 minutes

1	cup vegetable oil	⅔	cup cocoa powder
2	cups granulated sugar	½	teaspoon salt
4	large eggs	1	teaspoon vanilla extract
1	cup all-purpose flour	1	cup nuts, chopped, optional

- In large bowl, combine all ingredients except nuts, mixing well. Fold in nuts, or sprinkle nuts on top of batter before baking.

- Spread into a buttered 13 x 9 x 2-inch baking pan. Bake at 350 degrees for 25 minutes.

Yield: 2 dozen

Option: Caramel Sauce - Combine ¾ cup butter, 1 cup brown sugar, ⅓ cup light corn syrup in a heavy sauce pan. Stir over medium heat to dissolve sugar. Boil 2 minutes, do not stir. Remove from heat and stir in 3 tablespoons cream. Cool 5 minutes, and pour over brownies.

Sprinkle toasted nuts and/or chopped chocolate over the caramel.

Peppermint Fudge

Preparation Time: 15 minutes plus 2 hours chill time
Prepare ahead.

11.5	ounces milk chocolate chips		Dash salt
6	ounces semisweet chocolate chips	¼	teaspoon peppermint extract
1	14-ounce can condensed milk	¼	cup hard peppermint candy, crushed

- In a saucepan, over low heat, melt chips with condensed milk and salt. Remove from heat and stir in extract.

- Spread into foil-lined 8-inch square pan. Sprinkle with peppermint candy.

- Chill 2 hours until firm. Cut into squares.

Yield: 64 (1-inch) squares

Chocolate Macaroons

Preparation Time: 10 minutes ~ Cook Time: 10 minutes

2   cups granulated sugar
½   cup vegetable oil
4   eggs
2   cups all-purpose flour
1   teaspoon salt

2   teaspoons baking powder
4   squares unsweetened chocolate, melted
1   cup nuts, chopped
1   teaspoon vanilla extract
    Powdered sugar

- Beat together sugar and oil. Add eggs, one at a time.

- In a separate bowl, sift together flour, salt, and baking powder. Add to egg mixture. Stir in melted chocolate, nuts, and vanilla. Chill until firm.

- Roll dough into small balls and roll in powdered sugar. Bake at 350 degrees for 10 minutes. Do not over bake.

Yield: about 2 dozen cookies

Kourambiedes

Preparation Time: 20 minutes ~ Cook Time: 12 minutes

1   cup butter
½   cup powdered sugar, plus extra for
    coating
1   teaspoon vanilla extract

2¼ cups all-purpose flour
¼   teaspoon salt
¾   cup walnuts, chopped

- Mix butter, sugar, and vanilla well. Work in flour, salt, and walnuts until dough sticks together. Shape dough into 1-inch balls.

- Place on an ungreased baking sheet and bake at 400 degrees for 10 to 12 minutes or until set but not brown. While warm roll in powdered sugar. After cooling, roll in powdered sugar again.

Yield: about 4 dozen

Chocolate Truffle Cookies

Preparation Time: 15 minutes plus 1 hour refrigeration time
Cook Time: 10 minutes

---

4 ounces unsweetened chocolate, chopped	¼ teaspoon baking powder
6 tablespoons butter, divided into pieces	¼ teaspoon salt
2 cups semisweet chocolate chips, divided use	1 cup granulated sugar
½ cup all-purpose flour	3 eggs
2 tablespoons unsweetened cocoa powder	1½ teaspoons vanilla extract

- Melt unsweetened chocolate, butter, and 1 cup chocolate chips over very low heat, (or in a double boiler) stirring occasionally. Cool.

- Mix together flour, cocoa, baking powder, and salt.

- In a separate bowl, beat sugar and eggs about 2 minutes. Beat in vanilla. Stir in chocolate mixture, then flour mixture, and the remaining 1 cup chocolate chips. Cover and chill until firm, at least 1 hour.

- Coat hands with cocoa powder to prevent dough from sticking. Shape dough into 1-inch balls and place 2 inches apart on ungreased cookie sheets. Bake at 350 degrees until puffy, about 10 minutes.

Yield: about 50 cookies

Chocolate Walnut Biscotti

Preparation Time: 30 minutes ~ Cook Time: 1 hour and 50 minutes ~ Prepare ahead.

---

4 ounces semisweet chocolate, coarsely chopped	1 teaspoon baking soda
1 cup granulated sugar	¼ teaspoon salt
1⅓ cups plain flour	3 eggs
⅓ cup cocoa powder	1 teaspoon vanilla extract
	2½ cups walnuts, coarsely chopped

- Line a large baking sheet with parchment paper. Grind chocolate and sugar in a food processor.

- Sift flour, cocoa, baking soda, and salt together.

- In a large mixing bowl, combine eggs and vanilla. Beat well at medium speed. Switch to low speed and add chocolate/sugar mixture and flour mixture. When half-mixed, add walnuts.

- Form two logs on prepared baking sheet, spacing evenly. Bake at 300 degrees until almost firm to the touch, about 50 minutes. Let cool 10 minutes. Leave oven on.

- Slice each log ½ to ¾-inch thick. Place back on parchment paper, cut side down, and bake at 300 degrees for 25 minutes.

- Turn slices over and bake 25 more minutes, until dry. Cool on wire racks. Store at room temperature up to 1 month.

Yield: 2½ dozen cookies

New South Pralines

Preparation Time: 10 minutes ~ Cook Time: 10 minutes

1 cup butter	Graham crackers, broken into rectangles
1 cup light brown sugar	(enough to line 10 x 14-inch jelly-roll pan)
	1 cup pecans, chopped

- In a saucepan, cook butter and brown sugar, bringing to a rolling boil.
- Line a jelly-roll pan with graham crackers. Pour butter and sugar mixture over crackers. Sprinkle evenly with pecans.
- Bake at 350 degrees until topping boils, at least 10 minutes.
- Let cool on rack until lukewarm. Separate and continue to cool completely. Store in an airtight container.

Yield: about 4 dozen cookies

Nutty Cranberry Cookies

Preparation Time: 15 minutes ~ Cook Time: 8 to 10 minutes

2½ cups all-purpose flour	¾ cup brown sugar, firmly packed
1 teaspoon baking soda	2 eggs
1 teaspoon salt	1½ teaspoons vanilla extract
1 cup butter, softened	1½ cups pecans, coarsely chopped
¾ cup granulated sugar	8-10 ounces dried cranberries

- Combine flour, baking soda, and salt. Set aside.
- In a large bowl, cream butter and sugars. Add eggs and beat until light and fluffy. Add vanilla.
- Gradually add flour to butter mixture. Stir in pecans and cranberries.
- Drop by heaping tablespoonfuls onto buttered cookie sheet about 3 inches apart. Bake at 350 degrees for 8 to 10 minutes.

Yield: about 3 dozen cookies

Chocolate Chess Pie

Preparation Time: 5 minutes ~ Cook Time: 45 minutes

3	eggs	1	teaspoon vanilla extract
2	tablespoons cocoa powder	6	tablespoons butter, melted
1½	cups granulated sugar		Pinch salt
2	tablespoons all-purpose flour	1	unbaked pastry crust
4	tablespoons water		

- Put all ingredients, except pie crust, in a bowl. Mix with wire whisk until smooth. Do not overmix.

- Pour into prepared pie shell and bake at 350 degrees for 45 minutes. Cool. Wonderful plain or with fresh whipped cream.

Serves: 6 to 8

Variation: For Chocolate Almond Chess Pie, add 1 teaspoon almond extract and sliced toasted almonds for garnish.

Easy Apple Enchiladas

Preparation Time: 40 minutes ~ Cook Time: 20 minutes

1	21-ounce can apple fruit filling	½	cup water
6	8-inch flour tortillas	½	cup light brown sugar, packed
1½	teaspoons ground cinnamon	½	cup granulated sugar
⅓	cup butter		

- Spoon apple filling evenly down center of each tortilla, and sprinkle evenly with cinnamon. Roll up tortilla and place seam side down in a lightly greased 2-quart baking dish.

- Place butter, water, brown sugar, and sugar in a saucepan, and bring to a boil. Reduce heat and simmer, stirring constantly for 3 minutes. Pour over enchiladas and let stand for 30 minutes.

- Sprinkle more cinnamon over enchiladas. Bake at 350 degrees for 20 minutes. Let cool for 20 minutes. Slice enchiladas in half. Serve warm, with fresh whipped cream or ice cream.

Serves: 6

Next time, try peaches!

Fresh Blueberry Cream Pie

Preparation Time: 10 minutes ~ Cook Time: 35 minutes
Prepare ahead.

1 cup sour cream	1 egg, lightly beaten
5 tablespoons all-purpose flour, divided use	2½ cups fresh blueberries (1 pint)
¾ cup granulated sugar	1 9-inch deep pastry crust
l teaspoon vanilla extract	1½ tablespoons butter
¼ teaspoon salt	3 tablespoons nuts, chopped

- Mix sour cream, 2 tablespoons flour, sugar, vanilla, salt, and egg. Beat 5 minutes at medium speed.

- Fold in blueberries. Pour into pastry shell and bake at 400 degrees for 25 minutes.

- Combine remaining 3 tablespoons flour, butter, and nuts and sprinkle on top of pie. Bake 10 more minutes. Chill 2 hours before serving.

Serves: 6

Lemon Lust

Preparation Time: 15 minutes ~ Cook Time: 25 minutes
Prepare ahead.

4 eggs	½ cup butter, cold
2 cups granulated sugar	2 dozen small, unbaked pie shells
1 lemon, quartered (rind, seeds and all)	

- Put eggs in blender or food processor and beat thoroughly. Add sugar and continue blending.

- Add the lemon (remove a little of the peel from the ends if you prefer less tart). Blend. Cut butter into 8 pieces and drip into blender.

- Mix one last time, just until butter is incorporated. Pour into shells, lined on a baking sheet. Bake at 350 degrees for 25 minutes.

Yield: 2 dozen tartlets

Personal Pecan Pies

Preparation Time: 20 minutes plus 1 hour refrigeration time
Cook Time: 35 minutes

3	ounces cream cheese, softened	1	teaspoon vanilla extract
½	cup butter, softened	1	egg
1	cup all-purpose flour	1	tablespoon butter, melted
¾	cup brown sugar	⅔	cup pecans, chopped

- Mix cream cheese, ½ cup butter, and flour with pastry blender or fork. Chill dough for 1 hour. Press chilled dough into buttered muffin tins. Form crust around the edges.

- Mix together brown sugar, vanilla, egg, 1 tablespoon melted butter, and pecans. Pour into individual crusts, approximately ¾ full.

- Bake at 325 degrees for 35 minutes.

Serves: 12

These are lovely for tailgating and buffets and are also great in miniature muffin tins. Excellent with fresh whipped cream, brandied optional!

Sweetie Pie

Preparation Time: 15 minutes plus baking time for sweet potatoes
Cook Time: 40 to 45 minutes

2	cups baked sweet potatoes, mashed (may use canned, drained)	1	cup milk
		¼	teaspoon ground cinnamon
½	cup butter	¼	teaspoon ground nutmeg
¾	cup sugar	¼	teaspoon ground allspice
2	egg yolks, beaten	2	pastry shells

- Blend together hot sweet potatoes, butter, sugar, and egg yolks. Add milk and spices.

- Mix well and pour into pastry shells. Bake at 400 degrees for 40 to 45 minutes.

Serves: 12 to 16

Red Balentine's Famous Pie

Preparation Time: 20 minutes
Cook Time: 20 to 30 minutes

1½	cups sugar	1	teaspoon baking soda
2	tablespoons all-purpose flour	1	teaspoon salt
4	tablespoons butter	1½	teaspoons vanilla extract
3	eggs, slightly beaten	1	9-inch pastry shell, pre-baked at 425 degrees
1	pint buttermilk		for 8 minutes with pie weights

- Cream together sugar, flour, and butter. Add eggs, buttermilk, baking soda, salt, and vanilla. Mix well and pour into pre-baked shell.

- Bake at 425 degrees for 20 to 30 minutes, until light golden brown.

Serves: 6 to 8

When I was a child, my grandfather, Red Balentine, owner of Balentine's Cafeteria, would fix us his mother's famous buttermilk pie. He claimed it was a secret family recipe and the clientele that would dine with us would always ask for it. He wouldn't divulge it, but now, in his memory, we are happy to share it with you.

So Blue Berry Tart

Preparation Time: 30 minutes ~ Cook Time: 12 to 15 minutes
Prepare ahead.

3   tablespoons plus ¾ cup granulated sugar,
    divided use
½   cup plus 2 tablespoons butter, room
    temperature, divided use
1⅓ cups all-purpose flour

2   pints fresh blueberries, divided use
2   tablespoons cornstarch
¼   teaspoon salt
⅔   cup water
1½ teaspoons lemon juice

- Mix together 3 tablespoons sugar, ½ cup butter, and 1⅓ cups flour with a fork. Press into a lightly buttered 9-inch tart pan. Bake crust at 375 degrees for 12 to 15 minutes, until lightly browned.

- Mix 1 cup blueberries, ¾ cup sugar, cornstarch, salt, and water in a saucepan. Cook over medium heat, stirring until mixture becomes thick and clear. Remove from heat and stir in 2 tablespoons butter and lemon juice.

- Let cool and fold in remaining blueberries. Pour into tart shell and refrigerate for several hours.

Serves: 6 to 8

Pâte Brisée

Preparation Time: 15 minutes plus 20 minutes refrigeration time

2 cups all-purpose flour, loosely packed, plus flour to dust on rolling surface	½ cup chilled unsalted butter, cut into small cubes
1 teaspoon salt	¼ cup vegetable shortening
	3-4 tablespoons ice water

- Stir flour and salt together in a bowl. Cut in butter and shortening with a pastry blender or in a food processor until the consistency of cornmeal. Work quickly so that the mixture remains cool.

- Add water 1 tablespoon at a time, to hold the mixture together in a ball. Sprinkle the water on the flour mixture while tossing with a fork to distribute the water as evenly as possible. The amount of water needed will depend on the humidity of the day. Use as little of the water as possible to make manageable dough. Too much water makes pastry tough.

- Wrap in plastic wrap and chill at least 20 minutes. The dough can be frozen at this stage and when ready to use, defrost in the refrigerator.

- Flatten the ball on a lightly floured surface and roll it in all directions with a lightly floured rolling pin. Keep turning the dough in quarter turns to roll it into an even circle. Dust the surface and the pin with more flour, if necessary, to keep dough from sticking. If the dough cracks, paste it together with a tiny bit of water.

- For use as a prebaked pie shell, fill with pie weights, and bake at 400 degrees 10-12 minutes.

Yield: 2 crusts

Tart Tatin Americain

Preparation Time: 1 hour
Cook Time: 1 and 30 minutes to 2 hours

1   recipe Pâte Brisée, halved
    (freeze other half for future use)
½   cup plus 2 tablespoons butter, divided use
1½ cups sugar, divided use

6   Granny Smith apples, peeled, cored, and
    cut into 16 wedges each
3   ounces walnuts, chopped
¼   teaspoon cinnamon
2-3 tablespoons bourbon

- Make Pâte Brisée. Refrigerate 20 minutes.

- Use 2 tablespoons softened butter to coat a 10-inch glass pie dish well, being sure to coat the rim. Sprinkle ¾ cup sugar evenly on bottom of the pie dish.

- Arrange apple slices in a spiral, starting from the center to cover bottom of pie dish. Arrange slices straightedge down around the sides. Evenly place the rest of the apple slices on top of the bottom layer.

- Sprinkle walnuts over top, and sprinkle ¾ cup sugar and cinnamon over evenly. Cover with remaining butter, cut into pats and drizzle bourbon over top.

- On a floured surface, roll out Pâte Brisée to approximately ⅛-inch thickness in a circle slightly larger than the pie dish. Fold in quarters to lift to place on top of apples. Unfold. Roll edges in to fit the size of the dish. Cut small vents in the dough.

- Place in the top third of a 375 degree oven. On bottom rack underneath, place a foil-lined baking sheet to catch drips. Bake 1½ to 2 hours or until the filling has caramelized to the color of deep butterscotch. Remove from the oven to cool slightly on a rack.

- While still hot, loosen crust from the pie dish with a knife around the edges. Place a serving platter on top of the pie dish. Holding the edges of both pie dish and platter, turn them over so that the pie dish is on top and the platter is on the bottom. Shake downwards gently, if necessary, to loosen the filling from the pie dish.

- Let sit at least 5 minutes before trying to remove the pie dish. It will continue to loosen as it sits. Slice and serve with vanilla ice cream.

Serves: 6 to 8

This is an Americanized version of a traditional French upside-down apple tart.

Recipes for Children

Tots to Teens

Recipes for Children

Fruit Dip

Preparation Time: 15 minutes

---

8   ounces cream cheese, softened
1   8-ounce container strawberry yogurt
¼   cup strawberry jam

½   teaspoon cinnamon
    Fresh fruit for dipping, such as sliced
      bananas, apples, pears or strawberries

- Place cream cheese, yogurt, jam, and cinnamon in mixer bowl. Beat at low speed until smooth and creamy. Use as a dip with fresh fruit.

Yield: 2 cups

Fruit Pizza

Preparation Time: 30 minutes plus 24 hours to chill ~ Cook Time: 15 minutes

---

Crust

1¼ cups all-purpose flour
¾   cup whole wheat flour
1   teaspoon sugar
½   teaspoon salt

1   teaspoon baking powder
1   teaspoon cinnamon
¼   cup canola oil
⅔   cup whole milk

Filling

⅓   cup peanut butter
8   ounces cream cheese

3   tablespoons honey

Topping

2   apples, sliced, or 2 bananas, dipped in
      lemon juice

1   pear, sliced
½   cup raisins

- For crust, combine dry ingredients and stir in liquid. Knead 10 times. Press into a 12 x 14-inch pizza pan or a 13 x 9-inch pan. Bake at 425 degrees for 15 minutes.
- For filling, mix together ingredients and spread on cooled crust. Chill 24 hours.
- For topping, arrange fruit pieces as desired. Slice and serve.

Serves: 8

Fruit Leather

Preparation Time: 20 minutes ~ Cook Time: 6 to 8 hours
Prepare ahead.

Apple

1	30-ounce jar applesauce	1	teaspoon cinnamon
3	tablespoons honey		

Peach-Banana

1	18-ounce can peach halves, drained	1	banana

- Line 2 (10 x 15-inch) jelly-roll pans with plastic wrap, tucking excess under each pan.
- In a blender or food processor, blend ingredients until smooth. Spread evenly in pans. Place pans in oven preheated to 150 degrees and bake 6 to 8 hours until leather is firm and dry.
- Remove plastic and leather and roll while warm; twist ends to seal and then wrap again with additional plastic wrap. Store at room temperature or freeze.

Yield: 2 rolls

Snowy Party Mix

Preparation Time: 15 minutes

1	10-ounce package mini pretzels	2	cups salted nuts
4	cups Cheerios	1	pound M&Ms
3	cups Corn Chex	2	12-ounce packages vanilla chips
3	cups Rice Chex	3	tablespoons vegetable oil

- In a large bowl, combine first 6 ingredients; set aside.
- In a microwave-safe bowl, heat chips and oil on high for 2 minutes, stirring once. Microwave on high for 10 seconds. Stir until smooth. Pour over cereal mix, stirring to coat thoroughly.
- Spread onto waxed paper to cool and harden. Break apart and store in airtight container.

Yield: about 16 cups

Banana Strawberry Smoothie

Preparation Time: 10 minutes

1   ripe banana, peeled and cut in chunks
1   cup fresh strawberries, washed and hulled

1   cup cold milk
½   cup strawberry yogurt
4   ice cubes, slightly crushed

- Blend ingredients in blender until smooth. Serve immediately.

Serves: 2

Peanut Butter Shake

Preparation Time: 10 minutes

½   pint vanilla ice cream or frozen yogurt
¼   cup creamy peanut butter

1   cup cold milk
1   large ripe banana, peeled and cut in chunks

- Combine all ingredients in blender and process until smooth. Serve immediately.

Serves: 2

Trail Munch

Preparation Time: 10 minutes ~ Prepare ahead.

1   cup sunflower seeds
1   cup dried cranberries or dried cherries
1   cup golden raisins

1   cup butterscotch chips
2   cups dry roasted peanuts

- Combine all ingredients and mix well.

Yield: 6 cups

Snack Chex School Fuel

Preparation Time: 1 hour
Prepare ahead.

¾ cup packed brown sugar	4 cups Rice Chex cereal
6 tablespoons margarine or butter	4 cups Corn Chex cereal
3 tablespoons light corn syrup	¼ cup semisweet chocolate chips
¼ teaspoon baking soda	

- Cover cookie sheet with waxed paper.

- Microwave brown sugar, margarine, and corn syrup in a large microwaveable bowl, uncovered, on high for 1 minute; stir and cook 1 minute more, until margarine is melted.

- Stir in baking soda until dissolved. Stir in cereals. Microwave on high for 3 minutes, stirring after each minute. Spread on cookie sheet and cool 10 minutes.

- Microwave chocolate chips in a small microwaveable bowl on high for 1½ minutes or until chocolate can be stirred smooth.

- Drizzle chocolate over snack mix. Refrigerate 30 minutes. Break into bite-sized pieces and store in airtight container.

Yield: 8 cups

24-Hour Fruit Salad

Preparation Time: 10 minutes plus refrigeration time

---

1 8-ounce can pineapple chunks, drained	1 cup coconut, grated
1 11-ounce can Mandarin orange slices, drained	1 cup mini marshmallows
	1 cup sour cream

- Combine all ingredients. Cover and refrigerate overnight.

Serves: 6 to 8

Pretzel Salad

Preparation Time: 30 minutes

Prepare ahead.

2   cups pretzels, crushed
¾   cup butter, softened
4   tablespoons sugar
8   ounces cream cheese
1   cup sugar

1   12-ounce carton Cool Whip, plus extra for optional topping
1   6-ounce package strawberry Jell-O
2   cups boiling water
2   10-ounce packages frozen strawberries

- Mix first 3 ingredients together and press into a 9 x 13-inch dish. Bake at 400 degrees exactly 6 minutes. Cool.

- Cream together cream cheese, sugar, and Cool Whip. Spread over cooled pretzel layer. Mix Jell-O with 2 cups boiling water. Add strawberries. Chill until slightly thickened. Pour over cream cheese mixture.

- If desired, spread additional Cool Whip on top. Refrigerate several hours. Cut into squares and serve.

Serves: 12

Pineapple Cheese Sandwiches

Preparation Time: 20 minutes

16   ounces cream cheese, softened
1   8-ounce can crushed pineapple, drained well
¼   cup green pepper, finely chopped

2   tablespoons green onion, finely chopped
½   teaspoon seasoning salt
10   slices white bread, crust removed

- Beat cream cheese until smooth. Gradually stir in pineapple, green pepper, onion, and salt. Blend well.

- Spread on 5 slices of bread; top with other slices. Cut each sandwich into 4 squares.

Yield: 20 mini sandwiches

The Latest Snack

Preparation Time: 20 minutes ~ Cook Time: 8 to 10 minutes
Prepare ahead.

1 pound sausage	1 teaspoon dried basil
1 pound ground chuck	1 teaspoon oregano
1 pound Velveeta cheese, cubed	2 tablespoons pimento, chopped
2 tablespoons dried parsley	2 loaves party rye bread
½ teaspoon garlic powder	

- Cook the sausage and ground chuck, drain well, and crumble. Add Velveeta, spices, and pimento. Stir on low heat to melt cheese and blend.

- Spread on rye bread and place on cookie sheet. Bake 8 to 10 minutes at 400 degrees. Serve hot. May freeze before baking.

Yield: 1½ party loaves

Mini~Tacos

Preparation Time: 15 minutes plus refrigeration time
Prepare ahead.

16 ounces cream cheese, room temperature	½ cup sharp Cheddar cheese, grated
2 packages dry taco seasoning mix	1 medium tomato, chopped and drained
1 16-ounce container sour cream	¼ cup sliced black olives, optional
3-4 heaping tablespoons salsa (hot or mild)	Large bag tortilla chips
½ cup lettuce, shredded	

- Microwave cream cheese 30 to 40 seconds. Mix taco seasoning with sour cream; add cream cheese and mix thoroughly. Stir in salsa. Pour mixture into oblong serving dish.

- Top with lettuce, cheese, tomato, and olives. Refrigerate several hours, overnight if possible. Allow pan to stand 1½ hours at room temperature before serving. Serve with tortilla chips.

Serves: 8

Mom's Chicken Nuggets and Honey Mustard

Preparation Time: 1 hour ~ Cook Time: 30 minutes

2 pounds boneless, skinless chicken breasts, cut into bite-size pieces
1 clove garlic, pressed
Buttermilk

1½ cups flour
1 tablespoon seasoned salt
Deep fryer filled with canola oil

- Mix chicken, garlic, and enough buttermilk to cover chicken. Marinate for at least 1 hour- the longer the better.

- Mix flour and seasoned salt in a large zipper bag. Shake chicken in bag. Remove and fry in hot oil until golden brown. Serve with Honey Mustard.

Serves: 4

Honey Mustard

3 tablespoons mayonnaise
3 tablespoons stone ground mustard

2 teaspoons honey

- Mix all ingredients in a blender. Chill.

Easy Chicken Pot Pie

Preparation Time: 30 minutes ~ Cook Time: 30 to 35 minutes

1 whole chicken or 4 large chicken breasts	1 14.5-ounce can chicken broth
2 15-ounce cans or 1 29-ounce can Veg-All vegetables	½ cup margarine
	1 cup self-rising flour
1 10.75-ounce can cream of chicken soup	1 cup milk
1 10.75-ounce can cream of celery soup	

- Boil chicken until fully cooked or use pre-cooked chicken. Cut into bite-size pieces and place in 9 x 13-inch pan. Drain vegetables and pour over chicken.

- In a bowl, mix soups and broth; pour over vegetables. Melt margarine. Mix with flour and milk. Pour on top. Bake at 400 degrees for 30 to 35 minutes.

Serves: 6

Cream Cheese Mints

Preparation Time: 15 minutes

8 ounces cream cheese, softened	Food coloring
½ teaspoon peppermint extract	Granulated sugar
2½ cups powdered sugar	

- Blend together cream cheese and peppermint extract until smooth. Place mixture on a large sheet of waxed paper and work in powdered sugar with hands until mixture holds together.

- Add 3 drops food coloring and work into mixture. Form into small balls and roll in granulated sugar. Flatten with a fork. Dry at room temperature. Cover loosely and refrigerate.

Yield: about 6 dozen

South-of-the-Border
Chocolate Cake

Preparation Time: 20 minutes ~ Cook Time: 20 to 25 minutes
Prepare ahead.

Cake

2	cups sugar	1	teaspoon baking soda
2	cups flour	1	teaspoon cinnamon
2	sticks margarine or butter	1	teaspoon vanilla
4	tablespoons cocoa	½	cup buttermilk
1	cup water	2	eggs, beaten

Icing

¼	stick margarine or butter	1	box powdered sugar, sifted
4	tablespoons cocoa	2	teaspoons vanilla
6	tablespoons milk	1-2	cups pecans, toasted

- For cake, sift together sugar and flour. In a saucepan, bring margarine, cocoa, and water to a boil. Pour liquid mixture into sugar and flour mixture and combine.

- Add remaining cake ingredients and stir thoroughly. Grease and flour sheet pan. Pour mixture into pan and bake at 400 degrees for 20 to 25 minutes until done.

- For icing, bring margarine, cocoa, and milk to a boil. Add powdered sugar. Add vanilla. Mix in pecans. Ice cake after it has cooled.

Serves: 12

Cinnamon Logs

Preparation Time: 20 minutes ~ Cook Time: 15 to 20 minutes
Prepare ahead.

1 loaf white sandwich bread	½ cup plus 1 cup sugar, divided use
8 ounces cream cheese	½ cup butter, melted
1 egg yolk	1½ teaspoons cinnamon
½ teaspoon lemon juice	

- Remove crusts from bread. Roll each piece flat.
- Mix together cream cheese, egg yolk, lemon juice, and ½ cup sugar. Spread on bread and roll up into a log.
- Combine cinnamon and 1 cup sugar. Dip logs in melted butter and roll in cinnamon sugar mixture until covered with a thick coat.
- Freeze at least 1 hour or overnight. May cut logs into bite-sized pieces prior to freezing. Bake at 350 degrees for 15 to 20 minutes on cookie sheet.

Yield: 30 to 100 pieces

Goof Balls

Preparation Time: 45 minutes

1 stick butter	2 cups Rice Krispies
1 cup sugar	1 cup pecans, chopped
1 egg, beaten	Powdered sugar
8 ounces chopped dates	Coconut, grated
1 teaspoon vanilla	

- Melt butter in saucepan. Add sugar, then egg and chopped dates. Cook on medium heat for about 10 minutes. Stir while cooking. Remove from heat and add vanilla.
- Mix Rice Krispies and pecans. Pour into hot mixture and mix well. When partially cool, make into small balls, about 1 inch in diameter, and roll in powdered sugar and coconut.

Yield: 40 balls

Mom's Butter Cookies

Preparation Time: 1 hour ~ Cook Time: 9 to 15 minutes

1	cup butter	3	teaspoons vanilla
½	cup sugar	3	cups flour
1	egg	½	teaspoon baking powder

- Cream together butter and sugar. Add egg and vanilla and blend. Sift together flour and baking powder; stir in by hand. Chill dough thoroughly.

- Roll out thin onto floured surface. Cut into desired shapes. Place on an ungreased baking sheet. Bake at 400 degrees until delicately browned, about 9 to 15 minutes; watch closely or they will overcook.

Yield: 4 to 6 dozen

M & M Cookies

Preparation Time: 20 minutes ~ Cook Time: 10 to 12 minutes

1	cup butter, softened	1	teaspoon baking soda
1½	cups brown sugar, firmly packed	½	teaspoon salt
2	eggs	1	cup plain M & Ms
1	teaspoon vanilla	½	cup nuts, chopped
2¼	cups flour		

- Cream butter and sugar together until light and fluffy. Add eggs and vanilla and blend. Combine flour, soda, and salt. Gradually add dry ingredients to butter mixture and blend well. Stir in candies and nuts.

- Drop dough by heaping tablespoonfuls onto greased cookie sheets, 3 inches apart. Bake at 350 degrees for 10 to 12 minutes. Cool on cookie sheets for 3 minutes and remove to rack or countertop to cool completely.

Yield: 2 dozen

Sweet Dreams

Preparation Time: 15 minutes ~ Cook Time: 10 minutes

1	cup butter	1	teaspoon cinnamon
1½	cups brown sugar	1	teaspoon ginger
1	egg	½	teaspoon salt
1	teaspoon vanilla	1	12-ounce package semisweet chocolate morsels
2	cups flour		
1	teaspoon baking soda	1	cup powdered sugar

- Cream together butter and sugar. Add egg and vanilla.

- In a separate bowl, mix dry ingredients, except chocolate morsels and powdered sugar. Add dry ingredients to butter mixture and blend well.

- Mix in chocolate morsels. Refrigerate until firm.

- Roll into golf ball sized balls and roll in powdered sugar. Bake on ungreased cookie sheets for 10 minutes at 375 degrees. Let cool on cookie sheet for 5 minutes.

Yield: 2 dozen

Ice Cream Sundae Cake

Preparation Time: 10 minutes plus 3 hours freezer time

1	16-ounce container Cool Whip	½	cup pecans, chopped
⅔	cup chocolate syrup	1	box (12 count) ice cream sandwiches
1	12.25-ounce jar caramel sauce	2	7.25-ounce bottles chocolate shell

- In a lasagna pan, spread half of the whipped topping. Drizzle chocolate syrup and caramel sauce over topping. Sprinkle pecans evenly over top.

- Cover with a layer of the ice cream sandwiches. (Cut to fit pan, if necessary.) Spread the rest of the whipped topping over the ice cream sandwiches. Cover completely with chocolate shell (be sure to shake well first). Freeze at least 3 hours before serving.

Serves: 12 to 16

Munchable Playdough

Preparation Time: 5 minutes

---

1 cup creamy peanut butter
1½ cups powdered milk
½ cup honey

¼ cup cocoa
Decorative toppings (raisins, chocolate chips, M & Ms, nuts)

- Mix all ingredients thoroughly. Play and eat.

Blowin' Bubbles

Preparation Time: 5 minutes

---

2 cups warm water
2 tablespoons liquid detergent

1 tablespoon sugar

- Combine ingredients. Blow through bubble wand or a clean fly swatter.

Elephant Stew

Preparation Time: 2 months ~ Cook Time: 4 weeks

---

1 elephant
Brown gravy
2 rabbits (optional)

Salt
Pepper

- Cut elephant into bite-sized pieces. This will take about 2 months. Add brown gravy to cover. Cook over kerosene fire for 4 weeks at 465 degrees.

- This will serve 3,800 people. If more are expected, 2 rabbits may be added, but do this only if necessary, as most people do not like to find hare in their stew.

Serves: 3,800 + 4

Preserved Children

- Take 1 large field, half a dozen children, 2 or 3 small dogs, a pinch of brook, and some pebbles. Mix the children and dogs well; place them in the field, stirring constantly. Pour the brook over the pebbles; sprinkle the field with flowers. Spread over all a deep blue sky and bake in the sun. When brown, set away to cool in the bathtub.

Acknowledgments

The Friend's of St. Timothy's-Hale organization would like to thank everyone who donated, tested, and typed recipes, edited, organized, brainstormed, and marketed **"Carpools to Candlelight".** Over the past three years many people have donated their time and talents toward the success of this book and we are deeply grateful for all their efforts. The following is a list of the people to whom we are indebted. If there have been any omissions, please accept our profound apologies!

Mary Amundsen
Fran Armstrong
Donna Alvarez
M'Lou Anderson
Patty Asher
Susan Nifong Austin
Leza Aycock
Barbara Bailey
Mike Bailey
Rita Bailey
Kim Balentine
Rosemarie Balla
Temperance Bartholomew
Laura Bierer
Wendy Blackburn
Celeste Blankenship
Mary Boliek
David Bond
Pam Bond
Jane Bond
Merritt Scott Bond
Karen Bornhofen
Renee Boyd
Patricia Brady
Christine Brandt
Myra Brickell
Doris Brimmer
Beverly Brock
Karen Brockschmidt
Mary Beth Brown

Joanne Brown
Elizabeth Bulla
Pam Bunn
Marsha Burt
Karen Calhoun
Karen Campbell
Jane Cipau
Ann Clampett
Patricia Claypool
Elaine Clark
Alison Cleary
Gretchen Clifton
Lorraine Cooper
Nancy Creagh
Ruth Creech
Becky Crenshaw
Jane Crowley
Christopher Cudabac
Sophie Curtis
Lynn Daniel
Patricia Dean
Kerry Dearstyne
Chuck DeSmet
Shirley DeWispeleare
Lee Dicenso
Barbara Dobner
Gigi Donovan
Carol Wall-Ellis
Mary Fausch
Candice Lilley Ferguson

Bobbie Filip
Susan Finch
Jean Fisher
Carol Fogartie
Joan Fontes
Vicki Fritsch
Denise Garner
Judy Gay
Louise Geaghan
Cindy Gilliam
Margaret Goad
Cindy Godwin
Peggy Grady
Barbara Grambow
Deb Grove
Robin Gunter
Tricia Hadley
Sharon Hammill
Karen Harmon
David Henard
Cheryl Henard
Marian Hensley
Ellen Herting
Margie Hertzler
Ford Hibbits
Rosemary Hibbits
Lucy Hobgood
Leila Holmes
Celeste Honaker
Tamara Hoxie

Martha Hunt
Iris Hutcheson
Michaela Iiames
Carol Irvin
Ann Marie Isbell
Katherine Isbell
Lisa Ives
Betsy James
Debra Jenkins
Barbara Johnson
Amy Johnson
Gail Jordan
Maria Kazmierski
Helen Keegan
Rebecca Keegan
Barbara Kelley
Chris Kelley
Gayle Kennard
Anita Kerr
Brenda Kessler
Ginny Killinger
Katie Kingsbery
Irene Kistler
Rita Knish
Sarah Knott
Donna Kocur
Jamie Larsen
Shirley Duke-Leung
Terry Lewis
Deanna Lord
Janette Lucy
Libby Luther
Meg Mansfield
Debra March
Annette Marcussen
Danna Markoff
Sharon Mathis
Laura Mavretic
Elizabeth McFadyen
Anna McFarland

Susan McKeown
Katherine McVey
Sally Merrell
Janet Mildenberg
Anita Moore
Betty Moore
Sally Moore
Marsha Morgan
Barbara Murray
Ann Nelson
Stephanie Niemchak
Sharon Nix
Rebecca Oxholm
Sandy Pair
Allen Parham
Carla Pasi
Brenda Pawloski
Sherry Pearce
Martha Peck
Norma Pedersen
Sharon Perry
Diane Petteway
Jo Anne Piatt
Linda Piccola
Lisa Phipps
Ginger Porterfield
Debbie Potter
Susan Potter
Kay Poursine
Pamela Price
Chris Reiland
Nancy Rendleman
Edie Reynolds
Lynn Reynolds
Holle Riegel
Dixie Riehm
Debbie Robbins
Ann Robinson
Constance Russell
Richard Saleeby

Jackie Newlin
Sharon Samia
Charlotte Sanson
Rebecca Schultz
Laura Shafer
Linda Scott
Cynthia Seymore
Pandora Shaw
Linda Short
Pauline Short
Virginia Siefkes
Judy Sims
Susan Sinden
Laurie Sorge
Susan Stevens
Ann Strader
Dana Sullivan
Peggy Supinski
Stella Taylor
Carolyn Thaxton
Fayeson Tilley
Frances Tillson
Judy Todd
Kathy Tribel
Nancy Van Dyke
Debbie Vaughan
Joan Vess
Susan Vick
Katherine Vyborny
Gretchen Waldrop
Tommy Waldrop
Susan Ward
Aline Washington
Maud Whitaker
Vickie White
Janet Whited
LeeAnne Whitworth
Alice Wilson
Jayne Wood
Page Wrenn

INDEX

R

S

Cookbook Friends of St. Timothy's-Hale School
3400 White Oak Road
Raleigh, NC 27609
(919) 782-3331 Ext. 503

Please send me _____ copies of *Carpools*   @ $19.95 each _____

North Carolina residents add 6% sales tax   @   1.20 each _____

Postage & Handling   @   3.50 each _____

Name _____

Address _____

City _____ State _____ Zip Code

Checks should be made payable to *Friends of St. Timothy's-Hale School (Cookbook)*

Cookbook Friends of St. Timothy's-Hale School
3400 White Oak Road
Raleigh, NC 27609
(919) 782-3331 Ext. 503

Please send me _____ copies of *Carpools*   @ $19.95 each _____

North Carolina residents add 6% sales tax   @   1.20 each _____

Postage & Handling   @   3.50 each _____

Name _____

Address _____

City _____ State _____ Zip Code

Checks should be made payable to *Friends of St. Timothy's-Hale School (Cookbook)*

Cookbook Friends of St. Timothy's-Hale School
3400 White Oak Road
Raleigh, NC 27609
(919) 782-3331 Ext. 503

Please send me _____ copies of *Carpools*   @ $19.95 each _____

North Carolina residents add 6% sales tax   @   1.20 each _____

Postage & Handling   @   3.50 each _____

Name _____

Address _____

City _____ State _____ Zip Code

Checks should be made payable to *Friends of St. Timothy's-Hale School (Cookbook)*

- -

Cookbook Friends of St. Timothy's-Hale School
3400 White Oak Road
Raleigh, NC 27609
(919) 782-3331 Ext. 503

Please send me _____ copies of *Carpools*   @ $19.95 each _____

North Carolina residents add 6% sales tax   @   1.20 each _____

Postage & Handling   @   3.50 each _____

Name _____

Address _____

City _____ State _____ Zip Code

Checks should be made payable to *Friends of St. Timothy's-Hale School (Cookbook)*

Cookbook Friends of St. Timothy's-Hale School
3400 White Oak Road
Raleigh, NC 27609
(919) 782-3331 Ext. 503

Please send me _____ copies of *Carpools*   @ $19.95 each _____

North Carolina residents add 6% sales tax   @   1.20 each _____

Postage & Handling   @   3.50 each _____

Name _____

Address _____

City _____ State _____ Zip Code

Checks should be made payable to *Friends of St. Timothy's-Hale School (Cookbook)*

- -

Cookbook Friends of St. Timothy's-Hale School
3400 White Oak Road
Raleigh, NC 27609
(919) 782-3331 Ext. 503

Please send me _____ copies of *Carpools*   @ $19.95 each _____

North Carolina residents add 6% sales tax   @   1.20 each _____

Postage & Handling   @   3.50 each _____

Name _____

Address _____

City _____ State _____ Zip Code

Checks should be made payable to *Friends of St. Timothy's-Hale School (Cookbook)*